TRAVELLERS

LANZAROTE & FUERTEVENTURA

By
BARBARA & STILLMAN ROGERS
WITH PAUL MURPHY

Written by Barbara and Stillman Rogers with Paul Murphy,
updated by María Sanz Esteve
Original photography by Stillman Rogers

Published by Thomas Cook Publishing
A division of Thomas Cook Tour Operations Limited.
Company registration no. 3772199 England
The Thomas Cook Business Park, Unit 9, Coningsby Road,
Peterborough PE3 8SB, United Kingdom
Email: books@thomascook.com, Tel: + 44 (0) 1733 416477
www.thomascookpublishing.com

Produced by Cambridge Publishing Management Limited
Burr Elm Court, Main Street, Caldecote CB23 7NU

ISBN: 978-1-84848-170-1

© 2005, 2007 Thomas Cook Publishing
This third edition © 2009
Text © Thomas Cook Publishing
Maps © Thomas Cook Publishing

Series Editor: Maisie Fitzpatrick
Production/DTP: Steven Collins

Printed and bound in Italy by Printer Trento

Cover photography: Front L-R: © LOOK die Bildagentur der Fotografen
GmbH/Alamy; © Ian Shaw/Alamy; © Jon Arnold Images Ltd/Alamy.
Back: © Thomas Cook

Although every care has been taken in compiling this publication, and the contents
are believed to be correct at the time of printing, Thomas Cook Tour Operations
Limited cannot accept any responsibility for errors or omissions, however caused,
or for changes in details giv[...] the [...]
reliance on the informatio[n ...] the
author's views and experier[...] when [...] necessarily represent those
of Thomas Cook Tour Ope[...]

Contents

KEY TO MAPS

★ Start of walk

✝ Church

☀ Viewpoint

✈ Airport

▲ 277m Mountain

Introduction

To travellers used to lush tropical islands — or even to the two better-known Canary Islands — Lanzarote and Fuerteventura's barren volcanic surfaces may at first seem forbidding and unattractive. But this first impression fades quickly as the beauties of these virtually desert islands unfold. The glimpse of the long golden beaches against an ultramarine sea, or the first view of the mountains turning golden-rose in the setting sun, will make believers out of sceptics.

The further you look, the more you find to fascinate you here. The striking and inspired art and architecture of César Manrique and other modern artists have made the most of even the impossible black *malpaís*, turning dramatic black landscapes of volcanic rock into stunning public spaces. Even the innovative agriculture of the wine-growing areas creates pleasing patterns on the land.

The volcanic activity itself is interesting; where else can you feast on fish grilled over the heat from an active volcano? On both islands there are craters to climb, caves to investigate and strange, beautiful landscapes to explore.

The beaches are, of course, what draw the most visitors: long strands of golden sand stretching for many kilometres, or little secret beaches caught in coves between rocky headlands. Long, gently sloping beaches characterise the eastern coasts, while heavy surf pounds those of the west, creating havens for both surfers and sunseekers. These islands have some of the world's best surfing conditions.

> These islands enjoy a fortunate climate . . .
> they offer not only good rich soil . . . but also
> wild fruits to nourish people
> without work or effort . . . these are the
> Elysian fields of which Homer sang.
> **PLUTARCH**
> *Life of Sertorius 1st–2nd century* AD

Windsurfers, too, flock here for the steady trade winds that sweep across the Canaries. And the islands' location at the juncture of Atlantic, Mediterranean and Caribbean waters, in addition to crystal-clear sea, give it dive sites unparalleled in Europe.

In the midst of all this natural beauty, sports activity and opportunity to bask in the sun, it's easy to overlook the interesting history. Traces of the prehistoric inhabitants remain, and buildings from the first European conquerors of more than 500 years ago have been restored. Despite the influx of tourists, Canarians still enjoy their colourful traditional festivals, and invite visitors to join in the fun.

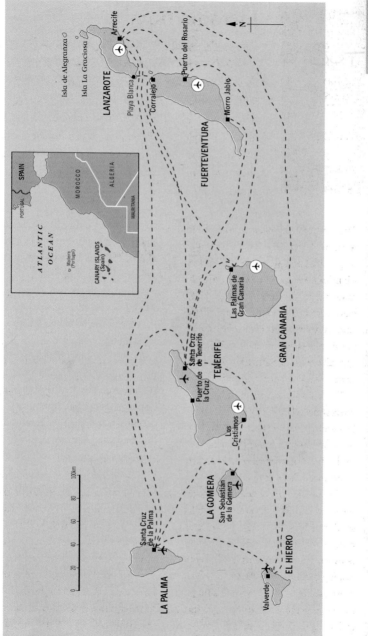

The land

The Canary Islands include seven larger and six very small islands, between 96km and 304km (60 and 189 miles) off the northwest coast of North Africa. From the easternmost island (Lanzarote) to the westernmost island (El Hierro), it is 496km (308 miles). West of El Hierro is open sea, all the way to the Americas.

The Canaries are Spanish territory, although the nearest mainland in Spain is 1,120km (696 miles) to the north. Geographically, the Canaries belong to Macaronesia (Blessed Islands), a larger group including the islands of the Azores, Madeira and the Cape Verde Islands. All of these share common volcanic origins, as well as common topography, fauna and flora.

Landscapes and statistics

But however much in common all these islands may have, Lanzarote and Fuerteventura stand apart from the rest for their shared climate (dry) and volcanic landscapes (largely barren). Unlike their neighbouring Canary Islands, these two present no lush tropical vistas, except in the artificially planted and watered environments in de luxe hotel complexes.

Each island is of volcanic origin and is dotted with volcanic cones, either long extinct or, on Lanzarote, still smouldering (*see pp52–3*). These volcanoes not only created the islands and shaped their terrain, but have also shaped the lives and cultures of the people who live there.

The larger of the two islands – and second largest of the Canaries – is Fuerteventura, which has an area of 1,731sq km (668sq miles). Its population, about 100,000, has more than doubled in the last decade, but is still lower in density than others of the Canaries group. Fuerteventura is also the oldest, and it is topographically less dramatic than Lanzarote, many of its volcanoes having been reduced by the erosion of 20 million years. Despite the thousands of years since its last eruptions, the island's surface is still largely barren, due to its very low rainfall.

Lanzarote is smaller, at 795sq km (307sq miles), with a population of around 135,000. Also very dry, especially in the south, Lanzarote does have areas made green by farmland, but very little natural vegetation. It was devastated in the 18th century by repeated volcanic eruptions, which left the southern part of the island with a lunar-like landscape. More of this island is covered by the black rough areas of 'fresh' lava flow called *malpaís* (badlands), while much of Fuerteventura is made up of sandstone, part of the sea floor thrust upward by the earliest eruptions.

Just off the northern coast of Lanzarote lies the small island of La Graciosa, along with the smaller islets of Alegranza, Montaña Clara, Roque del Este and Roque del Oeste. Just off the town of Corralejo, at the north of Fuerteventura, is Isla de los Lobos.

Lanzarote is divided into seven municipalities: Arrecife (the capital), Teguise, Haría, San Bartolomé, Tías, Tinajo and Yaiza, with most of its population residing in the south-central part of the island. Fuerteventura's municipalities are Puerto del Rosario, its capital, Pajara, La Oliva, Tuineje, Antigua and Betancuria.

It may at times be confusing to travellers to find addresses listed as one of the administrative municipalities, when an actual location is in a larger town some distance from the administrative centre. For example, Playa Blanca, a large resort town, is officially part of Yaiza.

Fuerteventura: Isla de los Lobos from Corralejo

History and politics

Following the end of the Franco regime, the Spanish government followed a policy of decentralisation. The Canary Islands became an autonomous region with two governmental centres, Las Palmas de Gran Canaria for the eastern islands and Santa Cruz de Tenerife for the western islands. Half of the regional government departments and the islands' Supreme Court are in Las Palmas and the other half of the departments and the Parliament are at Santa Cruz. Each has a Governor appointed by Madrid.

17–12 million years ago
Fuerteventura rises from the sea as a result of volcanic activity, the first of the Canary archipelago. Four million years later Lanzarote is formed in another volcanic eruption.

500 BC
The first settlers arrive on the islands. Believed to be Berbers, Maghreb or other Saharan peoples, they are tall, blond and blue-eyed. Originally a reference to the natives of Tenerife, the name Guanches was eventually applied to all of the native population (*see pp12–13*).

AD 1st–2nd centuries
Pliny the Elder, the Roman historian, mentions the islands, calling them the Fortunate Isles. He makes reference to Fuerteventura, calling it Herbania, a possible reference to the vegetation of the island.

c. 1312
Genoese seafarer Lanzalotto Malocello lands on the island he calls Tytheroygatra. His purpose there remains unknown, but the island is later renamed Lanzarote.

1339–42
The first mention of Isla Canaria appears on maps. Spanish vessels sail in search of the islands, though no conquests are recorded.

1402
Jean de Béthencourt, a Norman nobleman and a member of the Spanish Court, with the help of Spanish nobleman Gadifer de la Salle, sails under the flag of Henry III of Castile, intending to capture Gran Canaria

and Tenerife. Instead, he occupies Lanzarote and begins colonisation.

1404–6	Using Lanzarote as a staging post for reinforcements, Béthencourt sails to Fuerteventura and, within a year, succeeds in subduing the island, establishing his capital at Betancuria.
1488	The last of the Canary Islands is captured and Spain takes control of the entire archipelago.
1492	Christopher Columbus uses the Canary Islands as a final staging post before his voyage to the New World.
1494	The last battle with the Guanches is won by Spain.
16th–17th centuries	Sugar becomes the economic basis for Canarian wealth, followed by the development of vineyards and wineries.
Early 19th century	Islanders begin the cultivation of prickly pear cactus for the production of cochineal, a natural red dye extracted from a small parasitic beetle that infects the plant. It becomes a major export product until the introduction of synthetic dyes.
Early 20th century	Fuerteventura is ruled by landowners, who live on Gran Canaria.
1912	Self-government begins, in the form of Cabildos Insulares, with a governing body for each island.
1919	César Manrique is born in Arrecife, Lanzarote.
1924	Primo de Rivera seizes control of the Spanish government, and Fuerteventura, considered by the Spanish as the most remote and unattractive of all the provinces, becomes a place of exile for dissidents, most notably for the prominent educator and writer Miguel de Unamuno.
1936	General Francisco Franco, mistrusted by the Spanish government, is posted to Tenerife where he plans the military coup leading to the Spanish Civil War (1936–9). The islands quickly fall to his forces.
1950s	Tourism begins to become a dominant industry in the

Canary Islands and starts making inroads on Lanzarote.

1966 The first wave of tourism building and development begins on Fuerteventura.

1968 César Manrique returns to Lanzarote and begins his work to prevent the abuse of native culture and island landscapes that he sees occurring on the other islands. Monumento al Campesino is built and construction starts on Taro de Tahiche, his home.

1973 Mirador del Río at Haría is completed.

1974 Manrique's book on Lanzarote architecture, *Lanzarote, Arquitectura Inédita*, catalogues the importance of indigenous architectural form.

1976 Castillo de San José in Arrecife is converted by Manrique and becomes the Museo Internacional del Arte Contemporáneo.

1982 The Canary Islands become an autonomous region under the post-Franco constitution with government conducted jointly from the two capitals of Las Palmas de Gran Canaria (for the eastern islands) and Santa Cruz de Tenerife (for the western islands). The two provinces each have governors appointed by Madrid.

1989 The Canary Islands, as part of Spain, become full members of the European Community.

1990 Manrique opens the Jardín de Cactus at Guatiza, with more than 1,300 varieties of cactus.

1992 The Fundación César Manrique is formed and is based in his former home of Taro de Tahiche. Manrique is killed in a car accident.

2002 The Canary Islands adopt the euro.

2007 Inauguration of the Auditorio de Corralejo brings international music, theatre and dance companies to Fuerteventura.

2009 The Cabildo of Fuerteventura aims to get the entire west coast of the island considered a Natural Protected Area by the EU.

Haría City Hall

Representation and structure

The island Parliament is made up of 15 members each from Gran Canaria and Tenerife, eight from La Palma, eight from Lanzarote, seven from Fuerteventura, four from La Gomera, and three from El Hierro. In addition to its legislative role, the Parliament sets island budgets and appoints representatives for the mainland government in Madrid.

Each island also has its own island council, called the Cabildo Insular, which has a headquarters in the capital and holds certain powers of self-government. Although they are ultimately responsible for local services, these are delegated to *municipios* (regional municipal governments), then to town authorities, whose *ayuntamiento* (town hall) is usually a handsome traditional building in the central square.

The independence movement

While there is some demand for independence, it does not appear to be a popular movement. Visitors may see graffiti such as 'Spanish Go Home' or 'Godos Out', a reference (literally meaning 'Goths') to Spanish island workers, convenient scapegoats accused of taking jobs which locals believe should belong to them. The main party is the Coalición Canaria (CC), which usually carries about one-third of the popular vote. Its aims are moderate, directed towards greater autonomy rather than towards full independence.

The original islanders

When the first Spaniards visited these islands in the late 14th and early 15th centuries they found them settled by a blue-eyed, blond-haired people who greeted them as friends. Little is known of these people, but it is now believed that their ancestors were Berbers or other Saharan people who arrived there as early as 500 BC. Some scholars have suggested that there may have been two or more different waves of settlement.

They lived as Stone-Age peoples, making their homes in natural volcanic caves and simple stone-based huts. They were primitive farmers, surviving on a diet of fish, shellfish, goats' milk and meat, cheese and a roasted ground barley grain called *gofio*. They made pottery (examples of which can be seen in the museum in Betancuria; *see p116*) and basic tools of stone, wood, shells and animal bone. Clothing was made of goat skin, adorned with simple necklaces of shell and pottery. There is no sign that they used boats beyond simple paddle-powered dugouts for fishing and transport between islands. They mummified their dead (a rare piece of the burial covering is in the Museo Etnográfico Tanit in San Bartolomé; *see pp42–3*) and buried them in caves.

Pliny the Elder makes note of the settlers of these islands in reference to an expedition by the King of

Guanche mortar and pestle, Centro de Interpretación de Molinos

Mauretania, who found two kingdoms on an island he called Herbania (Fuerteventura). The northern Kingdom was called Maxorata and the southern Jandía, and they were separated by a low stone wall across the middle of the island.

Although visited by a Spaniard in the late 1300s, it was in 1402 that the Spanish King authorised a Norman member of his court, Jean de Béthencourt, to conquer the island now called Lanzarote. The neighbouring island of Herbania was soon conquered in 1405 and renamed Fuerteventura by Béthencourt. He immediately set about converting the islanders to Catholicism and repressing their native religion.

After the first peaceful encounters, the natives showed resistance to the conquerors and to conversion, and warfare between the two sides broke out. The Spanish also pitted native against native, taking advantage of tribal divisions and rivalries, so much of the fighting was between them. Soon after the conquest, captured natives were made the slaves of the new overlords and other natives married into their ranks.

The invading Europeans also brought disease with them, and it is believed that exposure to such diseases, as well as assimilation, is what probably brought an end to the native population. It has been estimated that within 30 years of the conquest most of the native people had disappeared as a distinct entity. Traces of the original peoples live on, however, in the descendants of the early relationships between the native population and their Spanish conquerors.

While you will hear the original natives of the islands referred to as *Guanches*, that name means 'Sons of Tenerife' and refers to the natives of that island. The term *Majos*, or cave dwellers, is also used for all native island people, while the natives of Fuerteventura were called *Majoreros* (a word that now applies to all residents of the island).

Guanche podomorph from Montaña Tindaya

Culture

The people who live on Lanzarote and Fuerteventura today come from many different places and represent a variety of lifestyles – farmers, craftsmen, resort managers, shop clerks and well-educated professionals. But those who grew up there, or have lived there for a long time, share certain cultural traditions with each other and with the residents of the other Canary Islands.

Guanche culture

It is unlikely that much of present-day Canarian culture is derived from the original inhabitants. Their language, dress, religion and other habits were extinguished by the conquistadors long ago, and Franco's policy of destroying any trace of pre-Spanish history here makes it almost impossible to paint more than a very sketchy picture of their society.

Spanish culture

Travellers expecting castanets and flamenco on Lanzarote and Fuerteventura will be surprised to discover that these are not traditional to the Canarian Islands. While you can see a flamenco show in a Caleta de Fuste nightspot, you can also find a Portuguese Fado singer performing nightly just up the street. Flamenco is just as exotic to the Canarian as it is to the British or German visitor, and the little girls' bright-red flamenco dresses sold in tourist shops are for tourists only. Even the cherished siesta is not observed by most shops, museums and businesses. The islanders may speak Spanish, but mainland culture is not necessarily their own.

In many ways Canarian culture is more like that of the South and Central American Spanish descendants. This may be because the Canary Islands, especially the less populated ones, have been treated more like colonies and developed the same sort of attitudes and relationships with Spain. Like their mainland and Latin American compatriots, Canarians have retained their love for fiestas, religious and otherwise, especially *Carnaval*, an excuse for each town to set up a stage for local talent and to schedule parties, sporting and musical events.

New influences

Without a doubt, tourism has changed the islands more than any force since the volcanoes. Along with the landscape, the fabric of island society has changed. While this is sometimes unsettling to islanders who see their culture being overtaken by foreign trends and local businesses giving way to international ones, most agree that the islanders are far better off with this new boost to their economy.

A continuing problem, along with the antagonism toward mainland workers who have come in to fill the better resort jobs, is the impact that the influx of people has on island ecology. But few question the fact that the desalinisation plants necessitated by tourism have benefited locals as well, or that money flowing in from tourists has built schools and hospitals and provided jobs for local families.

Forward-looking people try, as César Manrique did so successfully on Lanzarote, to encourage the development of communities and tourism, while protecting their heritage. They are proving that it is possible to combine local pride, character and integrity with profitable tourism. These are certainly exciting times for the islands. Money and modern ways beckon, but family roots and village loyalties are still strong. It's a delicate balance, and one that Lanzarote seems to have managed better than Fuerteventura.

Tile work and reed birdcages in San Bartolomé

Festivals

Canarians love parties, and the good news is that these are most often public affairs in which visitors are welcome to participate. Between religious holidays, island patron saint days, village saint days, city foundation days, a day to celebrate the repulse of an English pirate attack or a day to mark the miraculous discovery of an image of the Virgin – not forgetting the largest annual celebration, the two-week Carnaval – *it's a fair bet that some time during your holiday you will bump into at least one fiesta or* romería.

Celebrations typically include a procession, either secular (marching bands and fancy costumes) or religious (which may also be accompanied by bands and costumes). A *romería* (pilgrimage) can be a most colourful celebration, particularly when the statue of the local Virgin is paraded through the streets on a highly decorated cart pulled by two dressed-up bullocks. Sometimes celebrations are a combination of both. The streets come alive with musicians, and with food and drink vendors. Folk dancing, and sometimes Canarian wrestling (*see p157*), are staged. Fireworks often round off a fiesta, and revelries continue well into the small hours. Dozens of these fiestas, some quite small, dot the calendar. Ask at the tourist office about local events during your stay.

Carnaval

Although you may have heard about the gala week of all-night parties that fill the streets on the Canary Islands during *Carnaval*, be aware that these are on Tenerife and Gran Canaria, and that by comparison the celebrations on Lanzarote and Fuerteventura are positively subdued. This is not to say that they are not fun, colourful and exciting places to be, but don't expect the all-out explosions of Rio or New Orleans here. One thing tourists will appreciate is that these islands seem to schedule their celebrations so that people can attend several parties on different evenings. You may find buses laid on for these events, leaving from the major tourist centres. (Note that *Carnaval* here, unlike most other places, does not end with Ash Wednesday and the onset of the Lenten season, but may continue for a week or so afterward.)

These festivals take place only in those towns that have 'real' populations and traditions, not in the made-for-tourists complexes that have no native residents. On Lanzarote, one of the best is at Puerto del Carmen, where the grand stage is erected at the main plaza at the waterfront. Corralejo has a good celebration on Fuerteventura, although Puerto del Rosario and Gran Tarajal and other towns put on a good show as well. If you are visiting at another time of year, you can see exhibits of costumes and masks used for *Carnaval* at the Museo Etnográfico Tanit in San Bartolomé (*see pp42–3*).

A tradition still observed in Arrecife and elsewhere during *Carnaval* is the 'burial of the sardine' where an 8–10m (26–33ft) sardine made of cardboard or papier-mâché is pulled to the harbour or main square accompanied by mourners, invariably men dressed in black drag, 'weeping' theatrically. Then fireworks

FESTIVALS

Carnaval (**Carnival**) *February*

Semana Santa (**Holy Week**) *March–April*
Catholics walk their saints in a procession through the streets.

Corpus Christi *June*
This eight-day religious fiesta is the most important after *Carnaval*.

Romerías *June/July*

Virgen de la Peña *September*
Colourful pilgrimage with music festival on arrival in Betancuria, Fuerteventura.

Virgen de los Dolores *September*
Pilgrimage to Tinajo, Lanzarote, where an arts and crafts fair is held.

Carnaval mask, Museo Etnográfico Tanit, San Bartolomé

Local musicians perform for visitors

inside the sardine are set off, blowing it apart, and a display of fireworks follows.

Traditional music and dance

The idyllic image of men and women in traditional costumes dancing around the village square is just as dated in the Canary Islands as it is anywhere else in the modern world. But these customs are upheld by folkloric groups here, just as they are in other countries. These people learn the old dances and songs, play the old instruments and are willing to dress in traditional garb to share these old ways with neighbours and visitors. Every Sunday in Teguise a performance by such musicians and/or dancers is a highlight of the weekly market there. Performances begin about 11.15am, in the plaza next to the church, and include music, song and dance. Here you will see the old

Canarian guitar, called a *timple*, in use. The *timple* is still made in Teguise.

Hotels often have folkloric shows as part of their entertainment programme, and at Jameos del Agua music and dance performances are held three nights a week. You can sign up for a trip there with most island tour companies (*see p153*).

The arts

While neither island would compete with Paris or London for its art museums, Lanzarote has an active arts scene, and the entire island is a living showcase of modern art and architectural design. Much of the impetus for this came from César Manrique (*see pp34–5*), but his friends and fellow artists have continued the tradition he brought to the island. The result shows not only in two creditable art museums, but also in the number of local galleries where the works of contemporary artists are shown, admired and sold. In addition, you will find remarkable art in public places throughout both islands, from the lively and playful wind toys and other sculptures on roundabouts to Puerto del Rosario's outstanding public sculpture, and original artworks in restaurants, hotels and public buildings.

The primary art museums with permanent collections on Lanzarote are Museo Internacional del Arte Contemporáneo at Castillo de San José in Arrecife, and Manrique's own collection at Taro Tahiche, each containing works of foremost artists including Picasso and Miró. Private and public galleries with changing exhibits are Almacén in Arrecife, Galería Yaiza in Yaiza, and Centro de Arte Santo Domingo and Palacio de Herrera y Rojas, both in Teguise. Lagomar Restaurant in Nazaret has a changing display of sculpture and painting, while the restaurants El Risco in La Caleta de Famara and La Era in Yaiza have original art by Manrique and other artists. On Fuerteventura, Casa de los Coroneles in La Oliva holds temporary art exhibitions and the DUNAS short film festival in May. Puerto del Rosario, also on Fuerteventura, has adorned its streets and intersections with an exceptional collection of commissioned sculpture, and roundabouts on both islands often feature giant original sculptures. In addition, the Centro de Arte Juan Ismael (CAJI) holds modern art exhibitions, by both national and international artists.

César Manrique's house at Tahiche is built in traditional Lanzarote cubic style

Impressions

Since the 1970s, the Canary Islands have become as well known as the Spanish coasts for budget family holidays of sun, sea and sand. And the vast majority of tourists head straight for the better-known islands of Gran Canaria and Tenerife. While this type of holiday can be found in abundance in certain parts of Lanzarote and Fuerteventura, these resort areas do not make up a large percentage of the islands.

This means that a holiday here can be as lively or as quiet as the traveller prefers, and can have a good mix of sun, sports, culture, history and low-key relaxation. What you won't really find is the high-speed nightlife of many holiday resorts on Tenerife and Gran Canaria. All this adds up to a clientele of families and older visitors, without the frantic bar and singles scene that characterises many holiday destinations. To many holidaymakers, this is an attraction in itself.

Which island?

The key words for Lanzarote are volcanoes, modern art, small beaches, great resorts and quirky activities. The key words for Fuerteventura are beaches, surf, windsurfing and more beaches. If you shun resorts that seem overcommercialised, but like cultural and local life, Lanzarote would be the best choice. If your goal is beaches and water sports, and you don't expect to be entertained in the evening,

then Fuerteventura's laid-back pace is right for you. Better yet, you can easily sample both in one trip, especially if you choose a resort close to either Playa Blanca or Corralejo, where a short ferry ride will take you to the other island. In this case, you would do well to choose a self-catering holiday or a hotel with only bed and breakfast, which allow more freedom to move about without feeling as though you have paid for something you are not using. For the independent traveller there are many accommodation options on both islands in rural hotels and rural houses. These offer good-quality accommodation in wonderful sites. *Tel: 928 878 705.*
www.ecoturismocanarias.com

Island-hopping

There is little tradition of island-hopping in the Canaries, unlike on the Greek Islands. This is due to the distances involved, the packaged nature of Canarian holidays, which means few good budget hotels, and the packaged image of the islands, which in itself attracts a less adventurous type of traveller. But Lanzarote and Fuerteventura are exceptions to this rule, and they are so close to each other that even day trips between them are easy and inexpensive.

But you needn't be bound by the lack of a tradition. It is possible to reach any of the islands in under 45 minutes' flying time. Inter-island flights go via Gran Canaria for the eastern islands, and Tenerife (Los Rodeos, north airport) for the western islands.

Each island has its own airport. Fares are reasonable, check-in times are short, and it's an ideal way to sample another island for a day or two before deciding to commit yourself to a longer stay.

Boats also travel from Lanzarote and Fuerteventura to Gran Canaria, but this is a long trip and not a great saving. A better way to get there is to fly.

Fishing boats in the harbour at Puerto del Carmen

Getting to the islands

By far the majority of people coming to Lanzarote and Fuerteventura book a package tour that includes a hotel, and sometimes meals, along with the flight from their home country. Because of the cost of air travel, this may mean that they are getting their hotels for next to nothing. But the islands are well served by **Iberia Airlines** (*www.iberia.com*), which flies direct from Madrid to Lanzarote, offering connecting flights from London, from most major cities in Europe and from the USA. Lanzarote is now also served by scheduled flights with **easyJet** (*www.easyjet.com*), **Jet 2** (*www.jet2.com*) and **Monarch Airlines** (*www.monarch.co.uk*). Independent travellers arriving on their own will find car rentals, taxis and even buses to take them to their hotels. Lodgings in all the resort areas are easy to book on the internet, and very reasonably priced, especially for self-catering.

Car hire

By far the best way to get around either island is by car. There are bus routes, but the schedules are not frequent and they do not go to many sites a traveller would want to see. Not only is car hire inexpensive, it is readily available and competitively priced at all resort areas and entry points. On-site rentals are good for spur-of-the-moment plans and short rentals, but if you want to have a car for your whole stay, it is best to book ahead. **Alamo** (*www.alamo.uk* or *www.alamo.com*), which is represented locally by the island's biggest agency, Cicar, offers a wide selection of vehicles, with the security of knowing that a car will be waiting for you at the airport. When you step outside and see the long line of people waiting for the few taxis at the airport, you will be doubly glad you have car keys in your hand.

Driving

In the Canary Islands, as in mainland Spain, you drive on the right-hand side of the road.

The most immediate problem will be for those from left-hand-drive countries, such as the UK. In normal traffic, it will begin to seem natural as you follow other drivers. But at roundabouts or on roads with more than one lane, it becomes more difficult, because your natural instincts give you the wrong signals. Be especially alert and continue to remind yourself of this danger.

The most difficult time for some is in starting out in the morning on a road without other traffic. You can drive for some distance without realising that you are on the wrong side. To solve this, attach a card to your keys, with the words 'Drive Right!' printed in large letters. Whenever you leave the car, and need to pocket your keys, remove the card and tape it to your steering wheel. That reminds you as soon as you enter your car, at which time you return the card to your keys.

A roll of tape is a small price for avoiding a head-on collision.

In general, roads are new and in good condition, with comparatively little traffic. Motorcycles are very uncommon here, and drivers are generally courteous and careful. Mountain roads have guard rails. Unmade roads are not uncommon in the backcountry, but all resorts and towns of any size or importance are connected by tarmacked roads.

Travelling by boat

By far the easiest way of getting from Lanzarote to Fuerteventura or vice versa is by the ferry that shuttles between Playa Blanca and Corralejo, carrying cars and passengers. The trip takes less than 30 minutes, and in each case the

Hiring a car will enable you to explore the islands' fascinating landscapes

Montaña Roja, Fuerteventura

landing is a five-minute walk from the town itself. Even the buses connect with the boat landings, although there may not be one meeting every arrival.

Two lines run this service, leaving from neighbouring berths. They alternate times, between them providing an hourly service, from 7am until 6pm, except in mid-afternoon on weekends and holidays. Advance booking is usually not necessary, except around holidays.

Fred Olsen Line. Tel: 928 535 090. Naviera Armas. Tel: 928 867 080.

Day excursions (although you do not need to return the same day) to Fuerteventura leave from Puerto del Carmen on Lanzarote, via the glass-bottomed boat *Princesa Ico.*

Tel: 928 516 113. Sailing: daily, except Thur & Sun.

Cultural differences

Tourism is well enough established on both islands that you'll very rarely have a problem making yourself understood, or finding what you want. But don't assume that everyone speaks English. If you make an attempt to speak a little Spanish it will always be appreciated, and it's essential if you want to order something that is not on the menu, or buy an item that is not on view. A few words of Spanish combined with sign language will usually work quite well, and when all else fails, the hospitable locals will be happy to fetch someone who speaks English to translate.

Impressions

The old tradition of the siesta, while found occasionally, is certainly not the rule here. Museums, shops and many offices are open throughout the day, perhaps with a one-hour closing for lunch. In small villages, things may close down for the afternoon from around 1pm to 4pm, but apart from churches (which are often open erratic hours, if at all), places catering for travellers will remain open. Oddly, however, many tourist information offices close as early as 1pm or 2pm, and do not reopen until the next day (or at all on weekends).

The evening meal generally begins around 8pm, a little later than in northern Europe, though early by Spanish mainland standards. Unlike mainland Spain, however, restaurants

WHY 'CANARIES'?

The Canary Islands are not named after the tiny yellow bird that inhabits the islands. Instead, the birds take their name from the islands. The most enduring legend associated with the name of the islands is that they were named after native dogs (*canes*, Spanish for 'canines') found by the early Mauretanian explorers. Today's *verdino*, the native Canarian dog, is presumed to be a descendant.

open earlier and are happy to serve you an earlier meal. Locals eat their main meal at midday, so restaurants rarely serve a light meal at that time. For snacks and sandwiches, go to cafés or the village bar. They don't always have menus, or even food on display, but they'll usually be pleased to prepare you a snack.

Armas ferry at Morro Jable

Lanzarote

Lanzarote's startling volcanic landscapes would be fascinating enough in their own right, but it is what talented islanders have done with these that makes them unforgettable. This often violent surface of malpaís – *lava flow solidified into a craggy blackened jumble – is made hospitable by the smooth white walls of simple traditional buildings, combined with brilliant modern design.*

Lanzarote is fascinating not only because it is so visually striking. The ingenuity of its farmers and vintners has added to the volcanic landscape – not to mention the table – in very tangible ways. How Lanzaroteños have transformed a volcanic wasteland into an art form, and at the same time preserved its character and natural environment, is a story in itself.

In the Montaña de Fuego ('Mountain of Fire') the island's most recent volcanic eruptions have left a denuded land of contrasting colours, convoluted surface and still-hot cones. Preserved and protected as a rare example of unchanged volcanic surface, Timanfaya National Park is barely beginning to provide habitat for plants and small creatures. Bordering the island is a coastline alternating rough, jagged rock – sometimes rising in cliffs 500m (1,640ft) tall – with beautiful golden beaches. The sea that wraps the island in deep blue is unpolluted, and ranks as one of Europe's best diving waters.

Perhaps what distinguishes Lanzarote most clearly from other beach-rimmed islands is that its citizens have long valued their unique surroundings. No advertising boards disfigure highways, and few hotels are more than four storeys tall.

One man who had seen the fate of holiday havens elsewhere took the lead, and his neighbours listened. The multitalented island hero César Manrique (1919–92) preached an architectural gospel based on traditional building styles, indigenous plants and encouraging contemporary artists to work with the landscapes.

He set the example with his own giant 'wind toys' and with a series of natural/manmade attractions that have rightly become the must-see sights of Lanzarote (*see pp34–5*). The island is proof that man and nature

El Golfo
El Golfo
Los Hervideros
Salinas de Janubi

Punta Ginés

Playa Blanca

Punta de Pechiguera

can work together – or at least that man can create a joyous and appealing environment within whatever nature deals him.

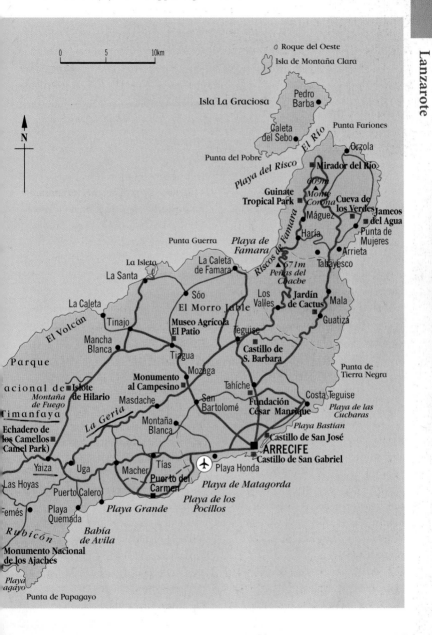

Arrecife and Puerto del Carmen

Once a pair of small, sleepy fishing ports on the island's east coast, Arrecife and Puerto del Carmen now have little in common except geography. Arrecife is Lanzarote's principal town (with about half the island's 110,000 population), while Puerto del Carmen is its principal resort (with about half its tourists). That said, don't expect either to be teeming with multitudes of people.

Port and airport

Both major points of arrival flank the city of Arrecife. Into its port, at the eastern edge, arrive ferries from Cádiz in mainland Spain, which call here once a week, and from Las Palmas, on Gran Canaria. Once each week, a ferry connects Arrecife to the capital of Fuerteventura, Puerto del Rosario – certainly not the best way for visitors to get there, since the trip from Playa Blanca is much shorter. The port, 3km (1³/₄ miles) from the centre, is on a bus route, or is a short taxi ride away.

Six kilometres (3³/₄ miles) to the west, almost to Puerto del Carmen and also connected to Arrecife by bus and an inexpensive taxi ride, is the island's airport. This attractive modern facility contains the island's smallest but most helpful Tourist Information Office, and the only one which covers the whole island.

Tourist Information, Lanzarote Airport, 6km (3³/₄ miles) west of Arrecife. Tel: 928 820 704. Open: Mon 8.30am–9.30pm, Tue 7.30am–9pm, Wed 8.30am–9pm, Thur 8am–9.30pm, Fri 8.30am–9pm, Sat 7.30am–9.30pm, Sun 7.30am–8.30pm.

Beaches

The coast on either side of Arrecife is bordered by long sandy beaches, most of them wide and roomy, sloping gently into the water. Each has its charms; those of Puerto del Carmen are backed by dark volcanic cliffs, and most are bordered by rocky outcrops at either end. Beaches at Costa Teguise tend to be smaller coves between rocky sections, apart from Playa de las Cucharas, the development's main beach. Those on the west end of the resort have the less attractive backdrop of Arrecife's port.

On the western end of Arrecife, but still right in the centre of town, is Playa de Reducto, a low-key strand with a long, level entry good for children. Just beyond the airport the serious beaches begin – the 12km (7¹/₂ miles) of sand that catapulted Puerto del Carmen into international resort status.

Costa Teguise

This large, new, made-for-tourists resort town, 7km (4$\frac{1}{4}$ miles) north of Arrecife, promises soon to outstrip Puerto del Carmen in size, although not in charm. Totally new and lacking in character, it is nonetheless a convenient place to stay, with beaches and dozens of resort aparthotel complexes at all levels of luxury and price. The water sports facilities are good (*see pp157–61*), and an 18-hole golf course is an oasis of green, at **Club de Golf Costa Teguise** (*Tel: 928 590 512. www.lanzarote-golf.com*).

Aquapark

The large complex near Costa Teguise has every water-related amusement park feature known to modern man, plus swimming pools, playgrounds, restaurants and shops. Children under 12 must be under adult supervision at all times.

Iglesia de San Ginés, Arrecife

Puente de Bolas, Arrecife

Avda. de Teguise. Tel: 928 592 128.
www.aquaparklanzarote.com.
Open: daily 10am–6pm.
Admission charge.

ARRECIFE

The capital has never attracted masses of tourists, except for shopping in its small shops, boutiques and some larger stores. Cafés and restaurants there are plentiful, and what it lacks in architecture, it makes up for in its castles, wide tree-lined waterfront promenade and in-town beach.

While from a distance the town's only high-rise looks out of place, up close the **Gran Hotel** is a striking and well-designed modern building, with the luxury of a large underground car park. Between the hotel and Charco San Ginés, the seafront is bordered by a wide and attractive **promenade**, with a small playground and benches shaded by arbours and tall trees.

Calle León y Castillo is the pedestrianised shopping street, running at right angles from the seafront near the elegant little bandstand and kiosk. Along with some attractive older buildings fronting onto the promenade, the tile-covered **Cabildo Insular** and the balconied building on the adjacent corner are among the architectural highlights of Arrecife.

Tourist information: Avda. Gen. Franco (seafront). Tel: 928 813 792. Open: (theoretically, if not in practice) Mon–Fri 8am–3pm. Better to stop at the more useful one at the airport.

Castillo de San Gabriel

On a small island off the centre of town, Castillo de San Gabriel is the focal point of the seafront promenade.

An earlier wooden fort built to protect the city from pirate attacks was replaced with a stone one in 1586, later reinforced as it appears today. **Puente de Bolas**, the bridge leading to it, is the symbol of the city.

Castillo de San José and Museo Internacional del Arte Contemporáneo

The late 18th-century castle was restored at the instigation of César Manrique to hold the acclaimed Museo Internacional del Arte Contemporáneo (Modern Art Museum), which includes works by Picasso and Miró. The sturdy old vaulted interior is an extraordinary setting for modern art. Be sure to go downstairs to admire Manrique's striking adaptation of the building. Just at the entrance to the fort, past the

Arrecife's ocean-front promenade

toy-sized drawbridge, a narrow stair leads up to the parapets.

North of town, just off the Costa Teguise road. Tel: 928 812 321. Open: daily 11am–midnight. Admission charge to museum; bar open 11am–midnight, restaurant 11am–11pm.

El Charco San Ginés

Now enclosed from the sea, the small harbour of little boats was the heart of the city in the early 1700s, when Arrecife's population stood at 17. The small bridge that crosses it was designed by César Manrique.

Iglesia San Ginés

The wide church, with its simple colonial façade and square tower, forms one side of the tranquil small Plaza de San Ginés, whose benches are shaded by trees. Inside the church, the statue of San Ginés (St Genesius) in the sanctuary is from Cuba.

Plaza de San Ginés, off Aquilino Fernández. Open: (theoretically, if not in practice) daily 9am–1pm & 5–7pm, except during services.

Aeronautic Museum

Before Lanzarote was important enough for its own airstrip, airmail was dropped off by parachute. This and other stories and artefacts bring early aviation to life in the little museum in the old airport terminal building.

Tel: 928 846 360. Open: Mon–Sat 10am–2pm. Free admission.

Fundación César Manrique

Just before his death in 1992, the artist César Manrique formed a foundation to manage and operate his home, Taro de Tahiche, as a museum of his work and his collection of works by friends. Built as a home in 1968, Taro de Tahiche became such an attraction that Manrique moved to a less conspicuous home in Haría. Under his guidance, the house has been carefully converted into a showcase of his work.

Surrounding the home are the contorted black stone lava fields from the 1730–36 eruptions, where Manrique planted native species of cactus and other plants, visible from the windows and balconies.

The exterior, above-ground portions of the building follow traditional stark white architectural styles, consistent with the style advocated in his definitive book *Lanzarote, Arquitectura Inédita*. Inside, an open passage leads down into a series of five sitting rooms, each placed in a rounded depression left by a volcanic gas bubble. These have central openings to the sky, and some have trees planted in the centre, under the opening. Seating is built into long, deep benches carved into the rock and covered with large, dramatically coloured cushions.

Each of the rooms is connected to the others by tunnels through the natural black stone, lined on the bottom with stark white, highlighted by concealed lighting. The ingenious use of natural elements with strong contrasts in colour and texture in the rooms and passageways is a trademark of Manrique's unique architectural style. Nowhere else did he have such an opportunity to play with nature as in his own home.

Particularly striking are the white and red parlours and the pool area, built in the bottom of an open volcanic *jameo*. Look for pieces of his sculpture and art in each room, especially *Woman and her Shadow* in the red room.

Upstairs, the galleries are laid out in his former living quarters and studio. Here, too, his skill at integrating art and nature shows, with a stream of lava literally flowing into a room through a window. In addition to Manrique's works are those by his peers and friends, Picasso, Miró, Chillida, Guerrero, Chirino and Sempere.

The foundation continues its mission to familiarise the public with Manrique's multifaceted work, and his desire to ensure that further development of Lanzarote avoids the pitfalls into which so many highly popular tourist destinations have fallen.

At the house there is a café, restaurant and bookstore where gift items are sold, including beach towels, silk scarves, ceramics and framed prints featuring Manrique's work.
Tahiche, 5km (3 miles) north of Arrecife.
Tel: 928 843 138.
www.cesarmanrique.com.
Open: winter, Mon–Sat 10am–6pm, Sun 10am–3pm; summer, daily 10am–7pm.
Admission charge.

Arrecife and Puerto del Carmen

The red parlour at the Fundación César Manrique

The living legacy of César Manrique

One of the great multitalented artists of the 20th century, Lanzarote-born César Manrique made a deep and lasting imprint on the island he loved. He was born into a comfortable Arrecife family in 1919, and spent much of his youth exploring the island, especially La Caleta de Famara on the northwest coast. The striking volcanic terrain and solid local architecture made a lasting impression on him, forming his artistic vision, which, in turn, shaped the future of the island.

Following his first exhibition at the Cabildo Insular in 1942, he exhibited in Madrid in 1944. He moved there in 1945 for further study and he became a major figure in Spanish art. In the mid-1940s he met and married Pepi Gómez, and their union lasted until her untimely death in 1963. Greatly affected by his wife's death, he moved to New York, holding three exhibitions at the Catherine Viviano Gallery there. While in New York, he met and became friends with such major American artists as Pollock,

Nature blends with art at the Fundación César Manrique

A Manrique mobile sculpture

unique attractions in different locations. At the height of his career and influence he died in a car accident near his home in Tahiche in 1992, aged 73.

Manrique's genius in art and architecture, as well as his vision for the future of the island, took shape in exciting wind-activated mobile sculptures (which he called 'wind toys'), stunning hotels, extraordinary architectural ensembles and visionary gardens and parks. Few since Michelangelo have matched the broad scope of artistic talent that forms the body of his work.

Rothko and Warhol, who added their influences to those of Néstor de la Torre, Henri Matisse, Pablo Picasso and other major 20th-century European artists.

His cultural roots eventually drew him back to Lanzarote permanently in 1968, where his drive, passion and extraordinary talents redirected the future of the island. Tourism, in its infancy at the time, was already seen as the island's economic future. Having seen the horrors of inappropriate development elsewhere, Manrique set a new environmentally and culturally sound path for Lanzarote's development. Utilising the nature of the island – its coarse hillsides, dramatic mountains and ragged lava flows – he created seven

THE MANRIQUE ROLL CALL

Manrique's major works can be found throughout Lanzarote and on Fuerteventura. Look for: Jameos del Agua in the Malpaís de la Corona, 1966 (auditorium, 1976–87); Monumento al Campesino, with the huge sculpture *Fertility*, Mozaga, 1968; Taro de Tahiche (Manrique home and Fundación César Manrique headquarters, Tahiche 1968); Restaurante El Diablo and Mirador, Timanfaya, 1970; Mirador del Río, northeast tip of Lanzarote, 1973; Museo Internacional del Arte Contemporáneo, Castillo de San José, Arrecife, 1976; Las Salinas Hotel, Costa Teguise, 1977; Jardín de Cactus, Guatiza, 1990; Restaurante La Era, Yaiza, restored ancient farmhouse. Throughout the island, at major road intersections, look for his unique wind-operated mobile sculptures (which he called *Juguetes del Viento* – wind toys), and at all the above attractions look for sculptured symbols in iron. On Fuerteventura the restoration and complex at El Molino in Antigua is his work, too.

PUERTO DEL CARMEN

Lanzarote's largest resort centre, Puerto del Carmen, differs from many of the built-for-tourism coastal towns because of its sense of place. Snuggled into the base of the hillside around the old fishing harbour, the original village plaza retains its community character. From the restaurants and cafés that surround the harbour side, visitors can watch local children playing at football and men at *bocce*.

From the harbour area, a new stone-walled walkway skirts the shoreline along the cliffs, providing sunset views and safe perches for gazing out to sea.

East of the harbour area (the town and its beaches stretch for 12km/7¹/₂ miles), connected by the seafront Avenida de las Playas, is Playa Grande,

Marina at Puerto del Carmen

and beyond it Playa de los Pocillos. Each of these beaches has its own full range of resort facilities.

The old harbour of Puerto del Carmen is 10km (6 miles) west of the airport. Tourist information: Avenida de las Playas (at the east end of Playa Grande). Tel: 928 513 351. www.puertodelcarmen.com. Open: Mon–Fri 10am–5pm.

Beaches

East of the harbour, along the hilltop overlooking **Playa Grande** (confusingly, until recently it was known as **Playa Blanca**), an attractive palm-lined promenade provides views and access to the beach below. One of the island's most attractive strands, Playa Grande is backed by high black lava cliffs, into which have been set wide stairways and small terraces planted with palms.

Facing the promenade from across the Avenida de las Playas are myriad shops, restaurants and bars. Amid the fish and chips, wiener schnitzel, Tex-Mex and Chinese restaurants, it's hard to find anything Canarian – or even Spanish – here.

A bit further east along the coast lies the expansive and sandy **Playa de los Pocillos**. One of the island's newest developments, this beach is considered one of the best; it is quiet (for now, at least) and safe for children because of its gentle incline. You can hire windsurfing equipment at the beach. Backing the beach is a full range of

Puerto del Carmen, the old harbour

resort facilities. Beyond, reached by the first seaward turning west of the airport, **Playa de Matagorda** is small and quiet, its clusters of low white cubic cottages set amid palms looking more like a desert oasis than a seaside resort. Both these are popular with inexperienced windsurfers, since they are more protected than other parts of the island.

Fishing port

The harbour, protected by a tall breakwater, is filled with small craft and colourful fishing boats. It is also home to several excursion boats, including the island's first glass-bottomed boat and another that makes all-day excursions to Isla de los Lobos and Fuerteventura (*see Boat trips, pp138–41*). The plaza overlooking the harbour, the Varadero, is the centre of activity for tourists and locals and the best restaurants are here.

Puerto Calero

The moneyed yacht set is evident at the stylish new marina that forms the nucleus of Puerto Calero. Cafés, restaurants and boutiques line the wide promenade that overlooks a sea of yacht masts. A whale skeleton dominates the upper plaza at the entrance to the new **Museo de Cetáceos de Canarias (Whale and Dolphin Museum)** (*Tel: 928 849 560. www.museodecetaceos.org. Open: Tue–Sat 10am–6pm. Closed: Sun & Mon*), which is interesting, but very pricey, in keeping with the resort's atmosphere. **Puerto Calero Galería de Arte** (*Tel: 928 511 505. Open: Mon–Fri 4–9pm, Sat 11am–9pm. Closed: Sun*) shows works by local and expat artists.
Marina tel: 928 510 850.
www.puertocalero.com

Central Lanzarote

Route LZ20 strikes off across the island from Arrecife, zigzagging northwest to end at La Santa, on the opposite coast, travelling through typical volcanic landscapes. At Mozaga it intersects LZ30, leading into La Geria, the island's wine-growing region. From Tiagua another road heads northwards to La Famara, a remote and scenic haven for surfers. To form a circular route, take the small paved road from La Santa to Sóo, and on to La Caleta de Famara.

LA GERIA

The entire landscape of La Geria, which lies to either side of the road connecting Mozaga and Yaiza, is one of black soil and stone walls, honeycombed with a neat, regular pattern of semicircular walls. This curiously pleasing black-on-black design is relieved by splashes of white *fincas* and the scattering of palms that surrounds them.

In places the walled depressions for vines form their pattern almost to the top of the volcanic cones that frame the valley. This ingenious cultivation (*see Malpaís to Malvasía, pp40–41*) has turned this valley into one of the island's most productive. Although the most familiar product is the distinctive Malvasía (Malmsey), the region also produces creditable red and white table wines. *Bodegas* (wineries) dot the route, offering samples of their wines, as well as interesting displays of old wine-making implements.

Bodega Suárez

Old winery tools decorate the walls of this family winery, where you can sample a variety of their wines in a low-pressure atmosphere.
Rte LZ30, 4km (2¹/2 miles) north of Uga. Open: Mon–Sat 10am–6pm, Sun 10.30am–3pm.

El Chupadero

This *finca* is what the traveller wishes more *bodegas* were like – a pleasant bar-café with heavy wooden tables and a terrace with knockout sunset views. At the southern end of the *bodega* trail, this is a perfect spot to watch the sun turn the sky orange against the stark black landscape, over a glass of local wine (the list is excellent) and well-prepared tapas. You can buy wine here, as well as local preserves made of cactus.
Rte LZ30, 4km (2¹/2 miles) north of Uga. Tel: 928 173 115. www.el-chupadero.com. Open: Tue–Sun 11am–midnight.

El Grifo Museo

This rather extensive museum is housed in the old *bodega*, and it is fun to explore inside the old tile-lined storage 'tanks' that now house exhibits. These include machinery and equipment for pressing, bottling, corking and labelling, and even a still for making *aguardiente*. It is easy to miss the complete barrel-making shop on a mezzanine above the first room. Grapes were once carried from vines to the *bodega* by camel, since camels were the traditional beast of burden here; look for the several types of container adapted to camel saddles.

Wines are sold by the half-glass in the *bodega*. El Grifo is the oldest still-operating *bodega* in the Canary Islands, and the griffin on their sign is by – you guessed it – César Manrique, who had a hand in adapting the old *bodega* to a museum, too.

Rte LZ30, 2km (1¹/₄ miles) west of Monumento al Campesino intersection. Tel: 928 524 951. www.elgrifo.com. Open: daily 10.30am–6pm. Admission charge.

The volcanic landscape of La Geria

Malpaís to Malvasia

Adversity often brings out man's best creative powers, and this was certainly the case in La Geria. Until the early 18th century, the valley was a rich, fertile farmland, but beginning in September 1730 a six-year period of volcanic eruptions covered southern Lanzarote with thick layers of ash and lava.

When the farmers returned to their land after the eruptions had at last subsided, they discovered that the black ash had its uses. These tiny rough cinders capture the dew that falls each night, carrying it directly into the soil around the roots of the vine. The coarse volcanic rock – *malpaís* – left by cooling lava also had a use, for building walls to protect the vines from drying winds, blowing sands and constant sunlight.

This accounts for the unusual patterned landscape that visitors see in La Geria valley today, as well as for some very good wines.

Clearing circles in the ash, farmers plant a vine in a depression in the centre of each, then surround each vine with the black ash. The ash gathers dew and moisture during the night and morning, providing the vines with the moisture they need. Short stone walls, up to 2m (6½ft) high, surround or partially surround the vines, protecting them from drying winds. Traditionally, these were circular or semicircular, although you will see some rectangular enclosures as well. Looking like dried wood in winter, the vines burst into leaf and fruit in spring.

The sight of entire hillsides of stone circles covering the black landscape is stunning, especially in summer when the bright green of the vines intrudes on the blackness. Throughout this uniquely patterned landscape are *bodegas*, where visitors can sample

Malvasia maturing

Wine production is important to Lanzarote's economy

and buy the wines, or simply learn more about their production at a wine museum.

Wine tasting is a popular activity with visitors

La Geria lies at the foot of Timanfaya between Yaiza and Tinajo. The best route to see the landscape and to visit *bodegas* is highway LZ30, which runs from Mozaga to Uga, on the outskirts of Yaiza. Another wine-growing region on the island is on the slopes of the northern shore, especially around the town of Ye, near Mirador del Río.

WINE TERMS

Tinto – red
Blanco – white
Rosado – rose
Seco – dry
Semi-seco – medium dry
Dulce – sweet

San Bartolomé and Mozaga

San Bartolomé was a centre for the island's earliest inhabitants, and later an inland refuge from pirate attacks. An attractive ensemble of buildings – a church with a tea-caddy bell tower, a theatre and a town hall – sits around a raised terrace with a fountain. Below, gardens spill down several more sets of terraced plazas, curiously devoid of the cafés that would fit them so perfectly. Opposite the lowest of these is the lovely 1735 home of a prosperous family, now the Museo Etnográfico Tanit.

Monumento al Campesino

At the roundabout where the La Geria road turns off, you can't miss the 15m (49ft) white cubist monument – supposedly of a farmer, his cat and a rat, although few people claim to make these out. The placement of this monument to the hard-working farmers – *campesinos* – is in the exact centre of the island.

Cactus gardens, bold white walls and the sharp contrasts of white against the black lava are characteristic of Manrique's vision for the island. In fact, the whole complex is classic Manrique: black lava in its natural flow and used as building stone, blindingly white expanses of wall with rounded edges, circular stone walls and structures, subterranean passageways, and gardens of native plants softening the rough, dark *malpaís* (volcanic rock).

Behind the restaurant is a patio of artisan studios. Large windows and open doors welcome visitors to watch, and you can buy the products of the weavers, leatherworkers, basket makers and tinsmith there. This **Handicrafts Centre** is hard to find – follow the upper walkway around the circular restaurant, or walk through the restaurant to see more of César Manrique's inspired design. In the patio, a stairway drops dramatically through the lava stone to a passageway in which pottery is displayed, leading to the restaurant. *Mozaga, 8km (5 miles) northwest of Arrecife. Tel: 928 520 136. Open: restaurant & centre 1–4.30pm, tapas bar 10am–5.45pm. Free admission.*

Museo Etnográfico Tanit

As usual in Spanish colonial architecture, the buildings of this fine former home are set around a series of patios, in this case (like the town itself) on various levels, ending at a garden. Exhibits here are so varied and so filled with objects that a thorough investigation could take hours. They explore nearly every facet of the life and history of the island, beginning with its prehistoric residents. The most important artefact in this group is a segment of woven reed used in funerary wrappings, but it is in the good company of several excellent early pottery pieces. The extensive former *bodega* of this *finca* home forms the main part of the museum, with displays featuring winemaking, clothing, music, farming, baskets, lace and needlework, cheesemaking, carnival and other aspects of traditional life. Upstairs is a collection of local furniture in a room setting. The small family chapel is off a second patio. A gallery guide in English is provided for visitors.

Calle Constitución 1, San Bartolomé. Tel: 928 522 334. www.museotanit.com (in Spanish). Open: Mon–Sat 10am–2pm. Admission charge.

Monumento al Campesino, positioned at the exact centre of Lanzarote

Tinajo and La Santa

Tinajo is typical of Lanzarote's architecture – small white homes with backyard gardens. Surrounding the town are small farms. In this region, the jable *soil is still volcanic, but more suited to traditional agriculture than the black* malpaís *of other areas. The variety of crops grown in this area is surprising – along with the ever-present onions are potatoes, sweet potatoes, peas, beans, maize and even tobacco. La Santa is almost directly north of Tinajo, on the coast.*

Ermita de los Dolores

In Mancha Blanca, 3km ($1^3/_4$ miles) south of Tinajo on the road to Timanfaya, is the small church of Nuestra Señora de los Dolores, more commonly known as Nuestra Señora de los Volcanes (Our Lady of the Volcanoes) because of a miraculous intervention during the six years of volcanic eruptions in the 1730s.

The story is told that villagers carried the image of the Virgin from the church to the nearby volcano, which threatened to engulf Mancha Blanca in lava, in the same way that other island towns had been destroyed. Within minutes of their placing the Virgin on the volcano, the lava stopped flowing and the volcano subsided (or, according to another account, the lava changed course). The church is the object of a colourful pilgrimage each year on 15 September, when people from all over the island walk from Arrecife to the church. The pilgrimage is accompanied by a craft fair.

La Caleta

For a sense of just how desolate the volcanic area around Timanfaya can be, and how isolated some of its communities are, follow the road west from Tinajo (the turning is just past the Co-op market) to La Caleta. It passes the steep slope of Montaña Tenezara, riddled with caves, before entering a wild and empty volcanic landscape. The road ends at a low area of rocky coast, under a fall of cliffs. Almost hidden beneath the steep shore just before the road's end is the tight cluster of white buildings that make up La Caleta.

La Santa

Set along a rocky low coast, La Santa offers a pleasant main street lined with restaurants. Those on the coast side have terraces overlooking the uneven black shore, where waves break against the rocks. This is a favourite place for locals and tourists to come for a weekend lunch of fresh seafood and to browse leisurely in the few shops. One of the

Ermita de los Dolores in Mancha Blanca

Canary Islands' few youth hostels is located near the town centre, but is only open for pre-booked groups (*Tel: 928 840 021*).

La Santa Sport

Secure (from what, one can only wonder) behind its gated walls, La Santa Sport looks more like a high-class prison, with its barbed-wire-topped walls and guard-tower corners, than the exclusive resort it is. Inside are extensive facilities for more than 30 different sports, from martial arts and boxing, to golf and diving. Sports figures come to its cosseted facilities to train when mainland weather prevents it elsewhere. The lagoon that almost separates La Isoletta, on which it stands, is perfectly suited for novice windsurfers, with a pleasant breeze, but protected from the full force of the wind. *Tel: (0161) 790 9890 (UK)*. *www.clublasanta.com*

Tiagua and La Caleta de Famara

Tiagua, set in a sloping landscape, is larger than it appears on a map, but anyone in town can point to its main attraction, Museo Agrícola El Patio. If you are making a circular route through La Santa, the road through Sóo to La Caleta de Famara from La Santa is unmarked and hard to spot. Look for it opposite La Santa Sport, just past the Youth Hostel.

La Caleta de Famara

The little beachside town is more spread out than most, at one end of a beautiful wide beach in a deep cove and with views of overhanging cliffs and Isla La Graciosa. To its east, the steep slope of **Peñas del Chache** mountain drops into the sea; no road continues along this impenetrable coast, so La Caleta de Famara is accessible only from south or west, across **El Morro Jable**.

The compound stretching up the hill is **Playa Famara Bungalows**; your eyes are not playing tricks; the bungalows are semicircular in shape. Although there seems to be no direct connection between this innovative architecture and César Manrique, the town does have connections with the artist, who often came here when he was a boy. **Restaurante El Risco**, right on the shore, has original paintings by him (which you can see through the window even on Thursday, when it is closed) (*see Food and drink, pp167–8*).

Apart from the seafood restaurants, water sports are La Caleta de Famara's main occupation.

Swimming here is highly dangerous because of strong currents, but the 5km (3-mile) sand beach offers some of the Canary Islands' best windsurfing and surfboarding. **Famara Surf** is the place for equipment hire and for bicycles. La Caleta de Famara is home to **Calima Surf Camps**, offering week-long or daily classes in surfing (*see Water sports, pp160–61*).

El Morro Jable

The farming town of **Sóo** lies in the centre of the rolling moor known as El Morro Jable, named after the light reddish sandy soil, which is known as *jable*. Herds of goats appear like moving patches on the moor, and you can often see farmers herding them along the roads to their corrals. The region is good for cycling, its roads rolling gently through farmlands green with low growth. From high points on the moor you can see La Caleta de Famara, La Santa and Isla La Graciosa.

Museo Agrícola El Patio

Before becoming a museum, El Patio was a major estate farm. The complex includes an 1840 farmhouse and outbuildings, two types of windmill, gardens, animal corrals (usually containing a camel) and museums of folk life and winemaking. The windmill's workings are all new, and it has an unusual number of windows at the top, also not original but designed to allow light in so that visitors can more clearly see how the mill operates. You can sample wines for sale here. Last admission is one hour before closing time. The English signage is excellent, interpreting local life and traditions and identifying the many tools, household items, photographs and historical artefacts that demonstrate how farming and rural craftsmanship are the foundation of island culture.

Echeyde 18, Tiagua, 12km (7½ miles) northwest of Arrecife. Tel: 928 529 134. Open: Mon–Fri 10am–5.30pm, Sat 10am–2.30pm. Admission charge.

The dramatic setting of La Caleta de Famara

Island agriculture

In an area where the average annual rainfall is minimal (11cm/4½in in Fuerteventura and 14cm/5½in in Lanzarote) one would expect hardly any agriculture, but quite the opposite is true. In addition to a flourishing wine industry, the islands have an active farming community that produces food for local consumption and even for export. When the land was devastated by volcanoes in the 18th century farmers learned that the black ash, called *lapilli* or *picón*, could help them grow their crops. The ash captures and holds water from dew, helping to supplement the low rainfall.

Farms on Fuerteventura and Lanzarote are almost always planted in small tracts or plots and are usually surrounded by walls of native stone and lava. These walls protect the crops from drying winds and blowing sand. Because some of the best farmlands are high in the mountains – especially those in the north of

Traditional farming methods are still used to this day

Lanzarote, where they can take advantage of that region's higher rainfall – these fields are frequently terraced. Several dozen of these fields may rise like stairs along a mountainside.

Flavourful sweet onions from both Fuerteventura and Lanzarote are a major Canarian export to Spain and elsewhere in Europe. Long, straight rows are pushed through layers of *picón*, leaving tall green stems rising amid rows of mounded black. Potatoes are frequently found in both large and small plots along the roadside. They are popular on the islands for use in the native dish *papas arrugadas*, 'wrinkled potatoes'.

Gardeners will also recognise beans, peas, tomatoes and lettuces growing in the fields, along with an unusual variety of maize, grown for use as a grain, looking stunted and low as it grows under protective stone walls.

Lanzarote's other main crop is less well known. It is cochineal, a bright red dye that is non-toxic and is used for a number of industrial purposes including colouring food and drinks. It is used, for example, to colour sweets, cosmetics and the Italian drink Campari. Once a major export, cochineal was largely replaced by artificial colourants, and demand declined. But recent fears that the artificial dyes may be carcinogenic

A wide range of crops is grown, from onions to aloes

have made the natural product more popular again. The dye comes from a small beetle that lives on the pads of the nopal species of prickly pear cactus. At the appropriate time the beetles are harvested, dried and shipped off for processing. Look for them on the large flat lobes of prickly pear, which you will find all over the island.

Montaña de Fuego

Some of Lanzarote's most dramatic and memorable landscapes are those in and near the National Park that protects the Mountain of Fire. The land has to be seen to be believed – an unearthly terrain of lava that solidified as it poured out of the mountain and then was cracked and broken by still-moving hot lava beneath it. Where the volcanoes met the sea, more surprising sights await – half a crater forming sea cliffs above a beach strewn with semi-precious stones.

Charco de los Clicos and El Golfo

The relentless Atlantic surf of the western shore at El Golfo has broken away the outer shell of an old crater, leaving only a tall, jagged sea stack facing an amphitheatre of striated lava cliffs. These cliffs are in rich colours and remarkable patterns.

At their feet is a beach with a green lagoon caught behind it. The lagoon is not visible to those who arrive at this spot from the south by car, the easiest access to the beach. For the best view down onto the lagoon, drive around the headland to the town of El Golfo, or cross to the other side of the beach and climb to a higher vantage point. The best time to visit these western cliffs is

GEMS ON THE BEACH

As the cliffs break away, with them come crystals of semi-precious green peridot that mix with the coarse sand. Peridots are semi-precious gemstones thought to be pieces of the earth's mantle (picture a layer thinner in comparison than the skin of an apple) that are carried out in the lava from a volcano. They were very popular in jewellery of the Victorian era. In shops all over Lanzarote, you will find necklaces made of drilled peridots, but you can collect a handful yourself on the beach at El Golfo.

You will rarely find peridots by just kicking through the sand or water-worn pebbles. Look in the coarse sand and tiny pebbles near the high-water line, stirring them with your fingers and looking closely to spot the tiny glints of green. Most peridots you will find are quite small, although larger ones are not uncommon.

The Mountains of Fire

in the afternoon, when the sun fills the crater and picks out its varied colours. It is a particularly beautiful spot at sunset.

El Golfo

The small town of El Golfo sits along a corniche beside the dramatic blown-out crater, and is known for its seafood restaurants. In fact, a cruise down its only street might convince you that this is its only reason for existence. Just to the left as the road turns into town, you can park your car to access a short path to the best view down into Charco de los Clicos. You can reach the beach from here as well, via a wide path down the edge of the crater wall.

12km (7¹/₂ miles) northwest of Yaiza.

The lava cliffs of Charco de los Clicos

Parque Nacional de Timanfaya/ Montaña de Fuego

On entering the park from Yaiza, few can resist stopping for a picture of César Manrique's striking metal sign with the volcanic cone rising in the background. It is possible to drive through the park for free, but to access Islote de Hilario (see below) you must pay admission and join a short coach tour. Wait at the gate for a parking space to become available at the top; taxis and coaches have priority. You are not allowed to leave your car in most of the park.

This landscape is quite new in geological terms, created by the continued volcanic eruptions between 1730 and 1736, which buried 11 villages (*see pp62–3*). The 51sq km (19¹/2sq miles) surrounding the epicentre were declared a national park in 1974.
National Park entrance is 7km (4¹/4 miles) north of Yaiza. Tel: 928 840 057/840 056. Open: daily 9am–5.45pm (last coach tour 5pm). Admission charge.

Echadero de los Camellos (Camel Park)

Of all the camel rides that are offered as tourist novelties on Lanzarote and Fuerteventura, this one is perhaps the most interesting, since it is along the side of the desert-like volcanic cone, while most others are simply around an enclosed corral. The ride is not long (about 15 minutes), although the wait during high season often is. At the car park is an information office and small museum with interesting examples of earlier camel saddles, including one with a water barrel mounted on one side. Signage is in English.
3km (1³/4 miles) north of Yaiza. Open: daily 9am–5.45pm. Info point open daily 8am–3pm, but not very helpful – a far better one is at the Museo del Visitante.

Islote de Hilario and El Diablo

Atop a small volcanic cone past the admission gate is a restaurant and park activity centre, where you board the 'Route of the Volcanoes' half-hour narrated coach tour showing some of the park's most interesting volcanic features. You will be directed to one of these coaches upon arrival. This is as far as visitors are allowed to take vehicles. Park guides demonstrate the power and heat generated just underfoot, where the temperature reaches 140°C (284°F) only 10cm (4in) below the surface. Dry brush thrown into a depression ignites, and water poured down a pipe bursts back out like a geyser. Inside the stunning building – a César Manrique design – is the restaurant **El Diablo**, a café,

Short camel rides are available for tourists

souvenir shop and open barbecue pit. Here visitors can watch as their meals are grilled over the heat from the volcano's core below.
Restaurant tel: 928 840 057. Open: noon–3.30pm, bar 9am–4.45pm.

Museo del Visitante

The outstanding museum explores the science of volcanology (with a cutaway model of a volcano), the earth's internal structure, tectonic plates and the Canary Islands' volcanoes, complete with an interactive relief map showing the ages and activity of all the archipelago's volcanoes. Exhibits on the island's past consider both natural and human history, including the fishing and tourist industry. The museum also explains and shows the various types of lava, rock and landscape you see on the islands. A very

good, although small, museum gift shop and a helpful information point are here, as well as a viewing platform built over a typical *malpaís* lava field.
LZ67, Mancha Blanca, 3km (1³/₄ miles) south of Tinajo. Tel: 928 840 831. Open: daily 9am–4.45pm. Free admission.

Montaña Blanca

Just outside the park boundary, reached by unpaved road from Tinajo, the caldera of Montaña Blanca is a classic volcanic crater, an almost perfectly round rim enclosing a deep centre. You can climb this quite easily, but to find the trailhead you should ask at the Visitor Centre for a park brochure in German or Spanish. The English version does not include trails. Because of the sharp rocks, boots or heavy-soled shoes are essential.

Walk: Fields of fire

To see the park's extraordinary volcanic features at close range and with a knowledgeable nature guide, you'll need to book as soon as you finalise trip dates. Only seven lucky people can make this thrice-weekly walking tour led by a guide from ICONA, the Spanish nature conservancy organisation. There is no charge, and anyone who is reasonably fit may go, but in high season they are often booked a month in advance. English is spoken, both in reservations and by the guides.

Start at the Visitors' Centre in Mancha Blanca.

Tours are given all the year round, on Mondays, Wednesdays and Fridays. The office is open 9am–3pm for bookings, 9am–5pm for information (*Tel: 928 840 839*). Allow three hours, including vehicle transportation.

1 Museo del Visitante

Before beginning the walk, a visit to this museum helps set the stage for

Landscape in Timanfaya National Park

what you will see (*see p53*). From here a van will transport participants to the start of the walk, just north of Yaiza.

2 Tremesana

The walk begins on the flank of Tremesana. This volcanic cone predates the 1730s eruptions, and vegetation has started to grow on its slopes. Tremesana is just below Montaña Rajada, site of the spectacular mirador visited on the 'Route of the Volcanoes' coach tour. Fig trees have been planted in stone half-circles like those used to protect the grapevines from wind. One of the stone half-circles is buttressed to prevent it from sliding down the mountainside.

The walk continues alongside the fissure.

3 Fissure line

If you have first visited the mirador via the coach tour, you will have looked into this great tear in the earth's surface, running from Montaña Rajada to Montaña Encantada and caused by exploding magma. As you walk, the guide will point out different types of lava, and the plants and fauna that manage to live in the National Park. You may see a locust blown over from Africa (not uncommon here), a rabbit, a hawk, or perhaps the vultures that nest within the park's boundaries.

4 The lava lake

Lava pouring from the fissure at speeds up to 70kph (43mph) formed a lake 5m (16¹/₂ft) deep here, which has long ago dried up. You can look down into the fissures, which reach to the bottom.

5 Volcanic tubes

Molten lava and the gases generated by volcanic explosions form tunnels as they move, trapped underneath the

more rapidly cooling surface. Guides will show you how to recognise these from signs such as yellow sulphur stains. When it is safe, you may have a chance to jump down onto one of these to hear the hollow echo as you land. These hollow tubes are called *jameos*, and you will see them used in other parts of the island, especially by the artist César Manrique, who built his home in one.

The walk continues past a quarry, where the ICONA vehicle will meet and return you to the Visitors' Centre. *Another, longer walk of about 9km (5¹/₂ miles) is occasionally offered, but you must sign up in person after arriving on the island. Only those who are in good physical condition will be accepted, since the hike is over rugged terrain. The route follows the coast, where the volcanic flow met the sea.*

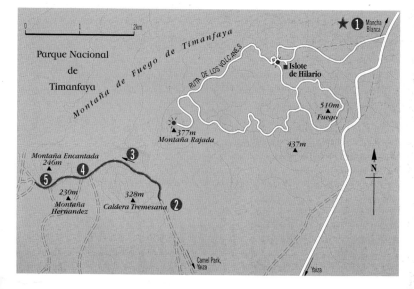

Southern Lanzarote

For those who prefer undeveloped beaches without rows of sunloungers, Lanzarote's southern coast is paradise. Beaches are not empty during the high season, but they are not backed by row upon row of apartment complexes, either. Monumento Natural de los Ajaches protects the high, rolling moors and the cliffs that enclose a series of beaches east of Playa Blanca. The sand is golden, and many of the beaches are set under tall, protecting headlands that cut the almost constant island winds.

Beaches

Right in the midst of Playa Blanca's busy commercial area, below the promenade lined with cafés and restaurants, a small beach sits in a natural cove. Another, **Playa Dorada**, is a 15-minute walk east and protected by breakwaters. To the west, on the other side of the port, the pleasant **Playa Flamingo** is similarly protected. The small **Playa de Montaña Roja** is at the far western end of town, not far from **Faro Pechiguera** lighthouse. These beaches close to all the hotels and apartment complexes become crowded quickly, so those with transport favour the undeveloped beaches of **Papagayo** and others at the **Monumento Natural de los Ajaches** (*see p58*).

Playa Blanca

Those who prefer the congeniality and amenities of a lively seaside resort will find them in the town of Playa Blanca.

Fishing village-turned-resort, Playa Blanca has made the transition with surprising grace. Parallel to its sloping main commercial street is the promenade and beach, lined with cafés and restaurants. Stone stairs lead from the port to both the shopping street and promenade levels, while the busy little harbour hosts car ferries and excursion boats to Fuerteventura and provides various other boat trips. West of this, an

SWIMMING CAUTION

Remember that the Canary Islands sit in the open Atlantic Ocean, surrounded by strong tides and currents. Swimming any distance from shore can be very dangerous, and at some beaches anything more than wading is unsafe. Never allow children to play on untethered floats except at well-protected beaches. Be alert to local conditions, asking local authorities and watching for beach flags (these are easy to remember, since the red, yellow and green colours mean the same as traffic lights). Every year, swimmers are lost in the currents; don't be among them.

attractive new esplanade is lined with palms and benches.

For those arriving by ferry, the port area offers car-hire offices (in the building to the left as you leave the port), buses to various parts of the island, and ample parking. Seven kilometres (4½ miles) west of the port area is Faro Pechiguera, the lighthouse; this entire shore and the mountainside behind it are fast being overtaken by developments. Most of these are low-rise, but are punctuated by the occasional grand complex, complete with neo-Moorish turrets.

In the other direction, past the two town beaches, the round tower of **Castillo de los Colorados** stands on the headland of Punta del Aguila. Built between 1741 and 1744, the tower was doubly useful; the bell in its little tower could be sounded to warn of approaching pirates, and, when the little drawbridge was lifted, making it difficult to storm, it provided refuge. A path leads along the top of the headland, a 25-minute walk to **Playa Mujeres**.

Playa Blanca is 35km (22 miles) southwest of the airport.

The coastline at Playa Blanca

Monumento Natural de los Ajaches

East of Playa Blanca, a little stone gatehouse where you pay a nominal fee marks the entrance to the reserve, where excellent signage leads to a selection of beaches. The first is **Playa Mujeres**, a wide stretch of golden sand where there are remains of an old limekiln. Easy-to-follow trails lead along the headlands and offer extensive views along the coast.

At the tip of the peninsula, the car park for **Playa Papagayo** sits atop a promontory with sweeping views across the sea to Isla de Lobos and the long stripe of startlingly gold sands at Corralejo. The little cluster of a

Water-worn rocks at Monumento Natural de los Ajaches

restaurant and two snack bar cafés overlooks the two beaches below, each almost hidden under tall, craggy cliffs. With one of the island's rare campgrounds (albeit a very drab one with no shade), nearby **Puerto Muelas** (also known as La Caleta) is popular for topless (or nude) bathing. If you are without a car, you can take **Princess Yaiza Taxi Boat** directly to Papagayo beach – and avoid the climb down and back to the car park.

Princess Yaiza Taxi Boat, Playa Blanca harbour. Tel: 928 514 322. Several daily departures.

Los Hervideros

A *jameo*, or tunnel-like bubble formed by lava and volcanic gases trapped beneath the surface, enters the sea here, creating deep sea caves and blowholes where heavy surf is further riled into continual froth. In rough seas, waves can break to the height of the cliffs. Well-designed walkways and stairs allow access to hollows and crevices, often directly above the sea, pounding in caves far below. These stairways are not readily seen, built of natural lava stone and blending right into the cliffs. The afternoon is the best time to go, when sunlight livens the black rocks.

Salinas de Janubio

Evaporating seawater for salt is one of the island's oldest industries, producing the salt used to preserve the catch of the fishing fleet, which once formed the backbone of the island's economy. The *salinas* at Janubio were among the largest of these saltpans and are impressive; viewed from above, they form a chequerboard of pans, separated by low stone walls, where the seawater evaporates to leave white squares of salt. The view is especially striking at sunset, when the pans reflect the colours of the sky.

Salinas de Janubio is 9km (5¹/₂ miles) north of Playa Blanca.

The impressive Salinas de Janubio

Yaiza

Whether Yaiza deserves its repeated nominations for 'Prettiest Town in Spain' may be questionable, but it is certainly attractive, especially entered from the east along LZ2, which is lined with palms and flower gardens. Make an extra turn around the roundabout for a better look at the creative recycling of a windmill, above the road.

Yaiza is 15km (9½ miles) north of Playa Blanca, 18km (11 miles) southwest of the airport. It has made a monumental effort to dress up its barren landscapes with gardens and plantings of palms, especially noticeable when entering from the east. The neighbouring village of Uga, on the road to La Geria wine region, is where the camels that give tourist rides in the National Park are bred, and at around 5pm every day you can see the long line of them returning home.

Ahumaderia Uga

While one might not immediately associate the Canary Islands with smoked salmon, this very highly regarded salmon smoker is in Uga. Fresh salmon is imported from both Scotland and Norway for smoking, and at the plant you can sample the product and buy it already packaged up to take home.
Rte LZ2, Uga. Tel: 928 830 132. Open: Tue–Fri 10am–1.30pm &
4–6.30pm, Sat 10am–2pm. Free admission.

Casa de la Cultura

This low white Canarian house often hosts exhibitions of art, but does not always keep its regular opening hours. Enquire here if the church is closed.
Plaza de los Remedios 1. Tel: 928 830 275. Open: (in theory) Mon–Fri 9am–1pm & 5–7pm. Free admission.

Galería Yaiza

This small private art gallery also houses exhibits of painting, sculpture, weaving and pottery, which are for sale.
Rte LZ2, Yaiza. Tel: 928 830 199. Open: Mon–Sat 5–7pm. Free admission.

La Era

More than three centuries old, the house at the core of La Era is one of only three houses left standing in Yaiza after the volcanic eruptions of 1730–36 (*see pp62–3*). Shortly after his return to

Lanzarote from New York, César Manrique (*see pp34–5*) and his friend Luis Ibáñez renovated the house, enlarged it, and converted it into a restaurant in 1968. His three paintings of island agriculture, wine and fishing – the last works in his 'Madrid style' – decorate its walls. Even if you are not dining there (*see p171*), you can look inside.

El Barranco 3. Tel: 928 830 016.
Open: Tue–Sun 11am–4pm & 7–11pm.
Free admission.

Nuestra Señora de los Remedios

Facing the square, the 1728 church is of particular interest for its painted altarpiece of white and gold, with blue alcoves, and for its painted ceiling.

Miniature village

For a month at Christmas, a little park in front of the church is devoted to a nativity scene with a miniature of the island's attractions, such as tiny fishing harbours surrounded by little white buildings, farms with small-scale plants, a lighthouse, Castillo and a saltpan made of pebbles, where the water is pumped by a tiny working windmill.

Lanzarote a Caballo

At the main road before the turning to Puerto Calero, this large riding centre provides camel, prairie wagon and pony rides for children and horse-riding trips to the volcanoes or shore for adults.

Rte LZ2. Tel: 928 830 038.
www.lanzaroteacaballo.com. Open: daily.

Nuestra Señora de los Remedios

The six-year eruption

On the night of 1 September 1730, the quiet rural life of the farming communities of central Lanzarote was altered forever. The earth itself seemed to become the enemy of the farmers and herdsmen whose homes made up the little villages. Three kilometres (2 miles) north of the village of Yaiza the ground opened up and rivers of molten rock began flowing over fields and villages. Mountains rose and lava continued to flow. With occasional respites, the volcanoes continued to erupt for the next six years.

The village priest of Yaiza, Father Lorenzo Curbelo, recorded the devastation in his diary. A month and a half after the initial eruptions he reported new ones. 'Enormous clouds of smoke escaped, flowing over the whole island,' he wrote, 'accompanied by volcanic ashes, sand and debris. The clouds condensed and dropped boiling rain on the land. The volcanic activity remained the same for ten whole days with cattle dropping dead, asphyxiated by the vapours.' Day by day he recorded the devastation levied upon his island as

The lava field north of Yaiza

The rugged volcanic landscape bears testament to the prolonged eruptions

he saw rivers of lava rush to the sea, then change course and overflow more and more land. He continued to record the disaster until the end of the following year, but the destruction continued on for five more years until April 1736 when the lava finally stopped flowing.

One by one, Father Curbelo noted the destruction of surrounding villages. By the time the volcanoes had stopped showering ash, deadly gases and lava over the landscape, more than 22 villages had been destroyed or severely damaged. Only a handful of buildings remained in Yaiza itself. This had once been a fertile land where cattle grazed and crops flourished. After the volcanoes it was a ruin, covered deeply in places with solidified rivers of black lava, and everywhere else with thick layers of pumice and ash.

Even today it is easy to see the magnitude of the destruction caused during those six years. Vast areas are still covered with lava and much of the rest remains black with ash. But farmers learned to adapt and use the ash, called *picón* or *lapilli*, to their advantage. The vast La Geria wine-growing area rose from the ruins and provided the island with a new industry, and elsewhere on the island crops grow through a covering of this black cinder.

Drive: Southern Lanzarote

Exploring the highlights of the southern tip of the island, this easy drive allows time for stops at the beaches that make this part of the island so popular. The trip may be broken into two sections, one on the way to the ferry to Fuerteventura and one on the return.

Start from Yaiza.

1 Yaiza

One of the most attractive towns in the Canary Islands, Yaiza maintains well-kept gardens backed by palm trees along its main approach, Route LZ2 (*see p60*). *From Yaiza, head east on LZ2, turning south at the Uga roundabout, 1km (²/₃ mile), signposted to Femés, 6km (3³/₄ miles).*

2 Femés

Tiny Femés perches at the saddle of the 600m (1,969ft) Atalaya de Femés. Iglesia San Marcial, built in 1818, has a collection of model ships inside. It was to Femés that the people of Yaiza carried their church treasures and kept vigil, praying for a miracle to spare their homes during the volcanic eruptions of the 1730s. Two restaurants and a belvedere offer views of the coast.
Leave Femés heading down towards Playa Blanca, turning left at Maciot after 1km (²/₃ mile). At the next roundabout (5km/3 miles), turn left and continue 2km (1¹/₄ miles) to the park entrance.

3 Monumento Natural de los Ajaches

Roads are well signposted to the beaches, the first of which is Playa Mujeres (2km/1¹/₄ miles). Popular with families, the beach is often decorated with sand sculptures. Playa Papagayo (3km/1³/₄ miles) is at the end of the peninsula, in an idyllic setting encircled by tall cliffs (*see p58*).
Return through the park entrance to the roundabout (5km/3 miles), turning left into Playa Blanca.

4 Playa Blanca

While the former fishing village has no 'must-see' sights, it is a pleasant place to stroll along the seafront, with plenty of restaurants and cafés (*see pp56–7*).
Head north on LZ2, signposted to Yaiza. Leave the highway after 9km (5¹/₂ miles), signposted to El Golfo.

5 Salinas de Janubio

Just past the intersection, the lay-by for viewing the saltpans below has no warning sign, so drive slowly to spot it (*see p59*).

Continue along the coast, where the road soon enters a malpaís of volcanic crumbles, an inhospitable and impenetrable rubble of rough, porous, black rock. Turn left to Los Hervideros (3km/1³/4 miles).

6 Los Hervideros

The rough, wild coastline of ragged black cliffs is at its most dramatic at this volcanic 'exhaust pipe' (*see pp58–9*). Be sure to explore the paths and stairways leading down to closer views.

Continue on to the turning to Charco de los Clicos, 3km (1³/4 miles).

7 Charco de los Clicos

Jagged cliffs form the inside of a volcano, one side of whose crater has broken away to form a deep, crescent-shaped cove. A short walk along a paved pathway leads to the beach, where you can gather peridots (*see p50*).

Continue around the headland, turning left to El Golfo (1km/²/3 mile).

8 El Golfo

El Golfo is a good dining stop, especially at sunset, although you should book ahead on weekends (*see p168*). Another reason to stop is to look down into Charco de los Clicos, following a short path from the left turn-off as you enter town, to see the green lagoon, fed by seawater from a subterranean source (*see p51*).

Leave El Golfo, continuing straight into Yaiza, 5km (3 miles).

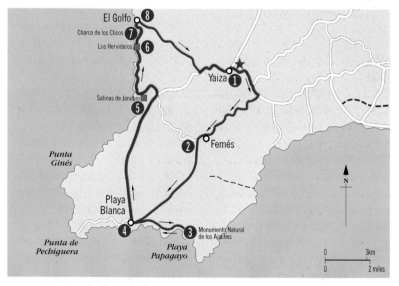

Northern Lanzarote

The 18th-century volcanic devastation wreaked by Timanfaya did not reach the northern part of the island, so the still-volcanic landscape is older and more weathered. But here the island's tallest mountains rise almost straight from the sea, and several miradors give stunning views of the coast and neighbouring islands. High in these mountains are farmlands still worked by hand, much as they have been for centuries. In this dramatic landscape are three of César Manrique's most dramatic works.

LOS VALLES AND GUATIZA

The little town of Los Valles sits under the long ridge of mountains that separates this valley from the sea. This is at the beginning of the region that receives Lanzarote's heaviest rainfall, and while that is still not a lot, it does make farming more successful here than in the drier areas.

A drive down into the town reveals an interesting sight – one of the main streets doubles as a runoff for heavy rains, with canalised sides and entries to homes sloping steeply up from its edges. Below the main road is the little Ermita Los Valles, and across Rte LZ10 is the small convent of Santa Catalina.

Ermita de San Sebastián

A secondary road (paved) crosses from Los Valles to Guatiza, passing close to the village of El Mojón, and its attractive little chapel with a stone arched doorway and sturdy buttresses. Beyond, close to LZ1, the road passes a patch of bizarrely shaped eroded rocks.

If you stop to inspect these you'll discover that they are formed of a conglomerate so unstable that it crumbles to the touch.

Jardín de Cactus

One of César Manrique's last works was to convert a disused quarry into a lovely garden of more than 1,400 cactus species. The quarry, where farmers had dug the volcanic ash they spread on the land to hold water, was a semicircular scar until Manrique envisioned it as an amphitheatre for displaying cacti. Nearly 10,000 cacti, ranging from tiny delicate plants to giants in fantastic shapes, grow among natural lava monoliths left in the quarry. A pool, walkways and terraces create a setting to show off these plants at their best. At the rim of the garden is a restored working windmill and, below it, a terrace café overlooking the entire garden. Visitors are encouraged to sit there and enjoy the view. A Manrique mural is above the bar, and, with

Manrique's curious Jardín de Cactus

typical Manrique humour, the 'sign' for this attraction is a spiny metal cactus, 8m (26ft) tall.

Guatiza, 17km (10¹/₂ miles) northeast of Arrecife. Tel: 928 529 397. Open: daily 10am–5.45pm (winter), till 6.45pm (summer). Admission charge. The bar & café are open 10am–5pm.

Parque Eólico

As interesting as the old windmills whose ruins dot the island are the modern turbines whose triple-bladed propellers harness the constant winds that sweep Lanzarote. A long row of these – 48 in all – stretches across a shoulder of Peñas del Chache, and the site has been enhanced by Luis Ibáñez, friend of, and frequent collaborator with, César Manrique. Gardens provide a foreground, and sweeping views across coastal towns to the sea provide a backdrop stretching to the beaches of Corralejo, on Fuerteventura.

Rte LZ10, 9km (5¹/₂ miles) north of Teguise. Open: daily, daylight hours. Free admission.

Haría

Local legend, for what it's worth, maintains that Haría is so studded with palm trees because it was a custom to plant one for the birth of each daughter and two for each son. Whatever their origins, these palms do give Haría the feeling of an oasis, tucked into a deep valley under the island's tallest mountain. Approaching from the south, the first view of it is as a green and white patch far below. Two plazas are within a few steps of each other, one with a white bougainvillea-draped terrace with a statue of a woman carrying a water jug.

The other, larger, Plaza León y Castillo is shaded by a line of tall trees that stretches in front of the church, **Iglesia de la Encarnación**. Inside the church is a sculpture of the Virgin by the Canarian sculptor Luján Pérez. This plaza is the scene of an excellent Saturday crafts market (*see right*). César Manrique moved to Haría after his Tahiche showpiece home became too popular with visitors for him to work there. *Haría is 15km (9¹/₂ miles) northeast of Teguise.*

Market

By far the best crafts market on the island is on Saturday mornings in Haría. All the vendors are local craftspeople or food producers, with no African imports so common in most island markets. The variety and quality are remarkable, from traditional needlecrafts and handmade dolls in local costume to stunning modern designs in all media. Appealing pottery cups have little mice hidden in the bottom or peering over the edges, sand-painting techniques are used to decorate modern-design photo frames, and jewellers work in local stones. A baker sells breads and biscuits, winegrowers and liqueur-makers offer samples, local women sell delicious honey cakes and you can buy goats' cheese by the 1kg (2¹/₅lb) wheel to take home. Uncrowded, friendly and reasonably priced, this is the market to visit for handmade souvenirs and serious gift shopping.
Plaza León y Castillo. Open: Sat 10am–2pm.

Mirador de Haría

The road into Haría from the south drops precipitously from the ridge of Peñas del Chache in a series of hairpin turns. Before it begins to drop, you will find a small mirador with a tidy white building, which provides a fine bird's-eye

Plaza de la Constitución in Haría

view into the leafy (for Lanzarote) valley. The town's white cubic buildings and palms look like a North African oasis and even some of the volcanic slopes that enclose it are green with farms.

Rte LZ10, 4km (2¹/₂ miles) south of Haría.

Taller de Artesanía Chiche

This crafts workshop is a fascinating place to watch an artist at work making glass beads and aboriginal ceramics.

Centre of town in Mager, Haría. Tel: 676 811 429.

View from the Teguise to Haría road

Teguise

Chosen as the site of the capital because coastal settlements proved too hard to defend, Teguise remained the capital of the island until 1852, when the coasts were at last secure from pirates. Designed by its early planners to have a grid of streets and wide plazas, Teguise retains the air of a colonial capital, filled with fine historic buildings in the colonial style, including two monasteries and a mountaintop fortress.

The stone-paved streets of the island's oldest town are a pleasure to stroll, marked by carved wooden balconies and doorways. They are uncrowded, except when Sundays bring half the island and all the tourists to town for the weekly market.

Teguise is 9km (5½ miles) north of Arrecife. Note that in Teguise (as elsewhere on the islands) opening hours are not necessarily as posted or published.

Castillo de Santa Bárbara and Museo del Emigrante Canario

The endearing quality of Lanzarote's castles is their diminutive size. This one adds location to its appeal, perched at the rim of a volcanic crater, also small, which you can enter using various trails. Views from the ramparts are extensive, enabling its 16th-century builders to watch for pirates arriving by sea. Inside, the Museum of the Canarian Emigrant relates the frequently sad history of mass emigration to South America, forced either by royal decree or grinding poverty. Displays and signage (in English) illuminate the hardships of island life that prompted people to leave, the journey and its dangers, household goods the emigrants carried and some of the successes these families achieved in their new homes.
1km (²⁄₃ mile) northeast of Teguise. Tel: 928 845 001. Open: Mon–Fri 10am–5pm, weekends 10am–4pm (in summer it closes two hours earlier & is closed on Mon). Admission charge.

Caja de Canarias

Caja de Canarias (Canaries savings bank) faces the same square as the church and Palacio Spinola. The building, which was built in the 15th century as a tithe barn, is of traditional style with two parallel roof ridges set on a square base. Just off the square, facing the church, is the entrance to

Iglesia Nuestra Señora de Guadalupe overlooks the Plaza de la Constitución

another old building you can look inside, a former mansion that now houses Restaurante Acatife (*see p171*).

Convento de Santo Domingo (Centro de Arte Santo Domingo)

A chapter of the Dominican order was founded here in 1698; look for the order's symbols carved in the stone crest over its door. The church is divided into two naves, and the altar of the main one of these has been removed altogether to make a stage. But the side altar to its left more than makes up for it, with gold-covered carving and polychrome wood figures and detail. There is also a fine wooden ceiling above this side altar. The church is now used for displaying temporary art exhibitions.

Calle de Santo Domingo. Open: Mon–Fri 10am–3pm, Sun 10am–2pm. Admission charge.

Iglesia Nuestra Señora de Guadalupe

The island's largest church befits Teguise's position as capital during the early years of its history. Built in 1680 as the seat of the diocese, the church has survived a number of pirate attacks, fires (the latest one was in 1909) and subsequent restorations. One particularly violent attack by pirates

Museo del Arte Sacro

nave style common to the islands, its two naves separated by arches. The main altar is baroque, as is the smaller one to its right; to the left is a small chapel. Only the church remains of the original convent complex, and it now houses a museum of religious art, but is difficult to find open.

Plaza de San Francisco.

Palacio de Herrera y Rojas and Palacio del Marqués

These stately homes, smaller than the Palacio Spinola (*see below*), are also built in the Canarian colonial style. The first, on Calle José Betancort, now houses an art gallery, where works of local and other artists are shown. The second, on Calle Herrera y Rojas, is now Patio del Vino, a wine bar and tapas restaurant whose tables fill the open patio.

Palacio Spinola

This large house, built in the mid-1700s, served for many years as the home of the island governor. Its furnishings are a mixed lot, some old, some more modern. But of the old homes that you can see inside, Palacio Spinola best preserves its original domestic appearance, with large rooms, woodwork and an interior chapel. César Manrique supervised its restoration in the 1970s.

Plaza de la Constitución. Tel: 928 845 181. Open: Mon–Fri 9am–3pm, Sun & holidays 10am–3pm (closes 2pm in summer). Admission charge.

is commemorated in the name of the street behind the church, Calle de la Sangre – street of blood. The church's somewhat mixed styles are partly due to its frequent restoration and partly to the happy blending of prevalent period architecture with the traditional Canarian building techniques.

Plaza de la Constitución.

Museo del Arte Sacro

The 16th-century Convento de San Francisco, also known as the Convento de Miraflores, is built in the double-

Restaurante/Museo Lagomar

Anyone who admires architecture that works in concert with the landscape and appreciates the work of César Manrique will want to stop at this restaurant to see how other architects have worked in this same theme. In this case, a stunning restaurant has been constructed into the red stone caves on a mountainside above the village of Nazaret. The cliff, eroded into fantastic shapes, is studded with little nooks and alcoves containing bars or just a few tables overlooking the landscaped pool. Restaurant proprietors are very welcoming to visitors, and the open-air exhibition space features the work of different artists each month (*for dining information, see p170*).

Nazaret, Rte LZ1, 2km (1¹/₄ miles) south of Teguise. Tel: 928 845 665.

Exotic plants decorate the unusual Restaurante Lagomar

Sunday market

Each Sunday morning, the spacious plazas of Teguise – Plaza de la Constitución, Plaza de San Francisco, Plaza Viera y Clavijo and Parque la Mareta – are filled with market stalls. These spill out from the squares into those surrounding streets wide enough to accommodate stalls and shoppers. There are some local crafts and wines on sale, but for the most part vendors sell the same things seen in street markets the world over: resale goods, gimcracks and cheap imports from Asia. That said, the market is lively, everything else in town (except the church and Museum of Sacred Art) is open, and the festivities and street performances are fun to watch.

Street performers run the gamut from the ubiquitous bronzed mime 'statue' to a Peruvian pan-piper playing 'I Can't Help Falling in Love With You' and selling his CDs – and drawing an appreciative crowd of tourists as though Peru were a town in southern Lanzarote.

At some time between 11am and 11.30am, costumed dancers and musicians assemble in Plaza de la Constitución for a half-hour programme of local dancing, accompanied by song and music on traditional instruments. While some resorts hold folkloric evenings and the occasional festival may include them, this market is the one place every holidaymaker can be sure of a chance to see local dancing and musicians during a week on the island.

A large tent in Plaza Mareta stages a 35-minute exhibition of Canarian sports, including a demonstration match of Lucha Canaria, the unique form of wrestling practised here. The admission price includes samples of Canarian wine and cheeses.
Parque la Mareta. Sun 9am–2pm. Admission charge.

Crafts at Teguise Sunday market

Shoppers crowd the Sunday market at Teguise

Although local crafts are hard to find on the street stalls, local shops remain open on Sunday, and at **Casa Kaos**, next to Palacio Spinola, these are showcased. Different artisans have spaces dedicated to separate displays of their work. Included are sand casting, peridot jewellery, elegant black volcanic rock jewellery, cactus jam and *mojo* sauces, ironwork, traditional and modern pottery, art glass and a wide variety of other items. This shop is one of the best sources of quality original local crafts on the island.
Calle León y Castillo 2. Tel: 928 845 597. Open: 9.30am–6pm.

In all the mass of shoppers and browsers, the only place in town where locals seem to outnumber tourists on Sunday is in the friendly little **Bar Cafetería Tahona**, a café and restaurant on Calle Santo Domingo (*see p171*).
Buses from all the major tourist regions provide transport to Teguise on Sunday. Parking is plentiful, in large car parks on the village outskirts. Keep going until you reach a car park without spaces, then go back to the previous one. There are many car parks, so it is not necessary to walk from the first one you encounter.

Walk: Teguise

Walking is the best way to appreciate the small architectural details – the doorways, chimneys and balconies – of Teguise's colonial buildings. As you walk, you will see many simple wooden crosses along the side of the street, which are covered in flowers every 3 May.

Allow one hour's leisurely walking time, plus stops.

Begin at Plaza de la Constitución.

1 Plaza de la Constitución

A graceful sloping square, Plaza de la Constitución is bordered on one side by Palacio Spinola, the former home of the island's governor. An old tithe barn is now Caja de Canarias.

2 Nuestra Señora de Guadalupe

Defining the opposite side of the plaza is the parish church, with its tall stone tower. The church has been the victim of pirate attacks and fires during its 300-year history.
Follow Calle San Miguel from the plaza's upper corner, stopping to look inside a former colonial home, now Restaurante Acatife. At the end, turn right into Calle de la Sangre, then left into Calle Herrera y Rojas.

3 Palacio del Marqués

On the left is a former patrician home, Palacio del Marqués, now housing a wine bar, its arcaded patio open to view.

Backtrack to the corner, turning left into Plaza de San Francisco.

4 Convento de San Francisco

At the far end of the plaza is the 16th-century Convento de San Francisco, whose buildings once extended the entire length of the square.
Turn right, crossing the square and following Calle José Betancort from the opposite side.

5 Palacio de Herrera y Rojas

On the right, just past Calle León y Castillo, the former noble home, Palacio de Herrera y Rojas, is now an art gallery.
Continue to Calle Santo Domingo, turning left.

6 Plaza Santo Domingo

Also known as Plaza Generalísimo Franco, this long palm-lined plaza is bordered by Convento de Santo Domingo, which is now used as an exhibition space for artists. A garden above the plaza has been recently transformed into a 'Lanzarote in Miniature' park, with tiny replicas of island landmarks.

Return along Calle Santo Domingo, turning right into the small plaza, then immediately left into Calle Correo. When this ends (notice the carved doorway), turn right into Calle Carnicería, then left into Calle Pelota, crossing Calle Timanfaya.

7 Los Árboles

The tiny charming street lined with trees looks much as it has for the past century, although the trees have grown taller. An old photograph is posted on the wall as you enter the street.

At the end, turn right into Calle Norte, then right into the plaza.

8 Plaza de la Reina Ico

The church of Vera Cruz forms one end of the plaza.

Peridot jewellery, a local speciality

Leave the plaza at the far end, turning right onto Calle Puerto y Villa de Garachico.

9 Galería La Villa

At the first corner is a small house set around a patio, now Galería La Villa. Inside, small shops are entered from the patio.

Turning left at Galería La Villa, walk along the side of Parque La Mareta.

At its end, a right turn through the archway takes you back to your starting point in Plaza de la Constitución.

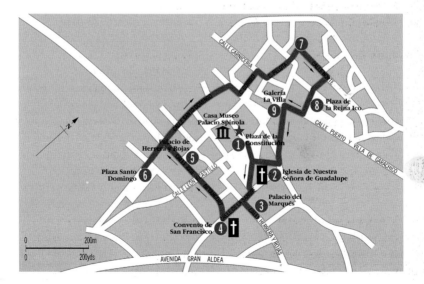

Drive: Los Valles (Teguise to Haría)

The drive from Teguise over the long ridge of Peñas del Chache and down into Haría's valley is Lanzarote's most impressive. Views of mountain and sea unfold as you drive, and a short side-trip into the farm-patched highlands leads to a tiny chapel and quite possibly the island's most spectacular viewpoint. Saturday is a good day for this trip, coinciding with Haría's excellent crafts market.

Begin at Teguise. Allow two hours' driving time, including stops.

1 Teguise

The former capital of Lanzarote maintains many of its proud colonial buildings, including a church, two convents and several noble homes. Atop the volcano, keeping a lookout for pirates, is Castillo de Santa Bárbara (*see p70*).

Leave Teguise, heading northeast on Rte LZ10 for 6km (3³/₄ miles).

2 Los Valles

This is a traditional agricultural village set in a lovely valley. Below the main road on the left, the little Ermita Los Valles sits in a quiet plaza. Notice the small convent of Santa Catalina alongside route LZ10 on the right.

Continue north on LZ10 for 2km (1¹/₄ miles) to a lay-by with views to the coast, continuing 1km (²/₃ mile) and turning right at the signpost for Parque Eólico.

3 Parque Eólico

A line of palms welcomes visitors to the impressive sight of the 48 modern wind turbines that catch the ever-present trade winds. It's worth stopping to appreciate the wonderful views over the surrounding landscape.

Return to LZ10 and continue north for 1km (²/₃ mile) to the turning signposted to Las Nieves. Follow the country lane through terraced farms for 2km (1¹/₄ miles).

4 Ermita de las Nieves

Small farms are terraced into the hillsides of these highlands, and it is not uncommon to see donkeys pulling a plough. The road ends at a flat shoulder just under the summit of Peñas del Chache; beyond this is thin air, as the mountain drops away suddenly in jagged cliffs. Far below, the town and the long golden beach of La Caleta de Famara border the sea. The view is phenomenal, with the town almost straight below, the shore of Isla La Graciosa and the knife-

edge of Peñas del Chache dropping into the sea. The little chapel is the site of a pilgrimage on 5 August each year.
Mass is celebrated at 5.30pm on the 2nd and 4th Friday of each month. Return to the main road, continuing north 2km (1¹/₄ miles) to a lay-by (the approach is hidden, so watch for it).

5 Mirador de Haría

Haría lies in a green valley below. The well-surfaced road drops in a series of parallel levels connected by sharp turns, but traffic is usually sparse.
Continue north to Haría, 4km (2¹/₂ miles).

6 Haría

Although most would not describe Haría as lush, its palms and gardens do distinguish it from much of the rest of the island. No wonder artists and craftsmen choose it as a home; visit them at the Saturday market (*see p68*).

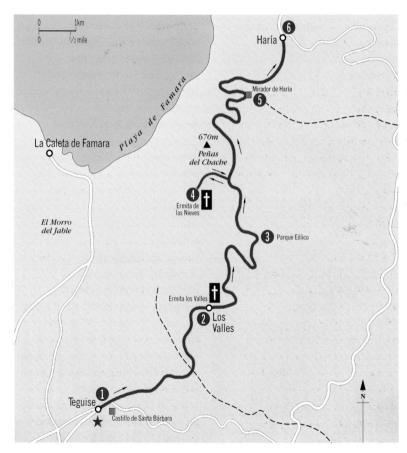

THE NORTH COAST

The northern tip of the island is varied in scenery, with the volcano of Monte Corona rising at its centre. High on its slopes are farms and a small wine-producing region. Three of the island's major sites are here, showing off the north's dramatic natural environment.

Mirador del Río

Trust César Manrique to take a former gun battery from the 1898 Spanish-American War and turn it into one of the island's top destinations. The view it reveals needed no artistic enhancements, extending across the Río – the channel separating Isla La Graciosa from the mainland – to the island and the islets beyond. The view of La Graciosa's little harbour is so clear that you can watch the excursion boats go in and out like little toys in a tub. The corniche into which the Mirador del Río is carved is caught midway in a jagged vertical cliff face about 450m (1,480ft) above the shore. Directly below is one of the old saltpans used for collecting sea salt. Outdoor viewpoints are made safe by thick walls of natural stone, and the restaurant-bar is almost hidden in the cliff, its curving windows looking out upon the view. Here the focus is on the view and the setting, with minimal architectural features apart from a stairway spiralling up to the top level.

9km (5½ miles) north of Haría.
Tel: 928 526 548. Open: daily
10am–5.45pm. Admission charge.
The bar & café are open 10am–5pm.

Mirador del Río

Orzola

The northernmost town on the island, Orzola spreads around its harbour, with seaside restaurants overlooking the water. Far from a resort, it is a little outpost fishing town where the fishermen seem to have traded in their oilskins for chefs' aprons. Boats leave from the quay for the nearby island, La Graciosa. West of town, accessed by a rough track, is the large beach, **Playa de la Cantería**, almost directly under the end of the long mountain that forms the spine of the island's northern end. Although remote and beautiful here, it is windy and dangerous for swimming because of the strong channel currents. The strong winds, however, make it popular with windsurfers. Safer – although one should always be careful of open ocean beaches – and easier to get to are those in the coves east of Orzola. Before reaching Orzola, you will pass the small **Parque Pardelas**, with donkey rides for children and a restaurant serving traditional dishes. *2km (1¹/₄ miles) south of Orzola. Tel: 928 842 545. Open: daily 10am–7pm. Admission charge to visit animals.*

Guinate Tropical Park

In a leafy compound, just before the escarpment of La Corona drops into the sea, live more than 1,300 exotic birds and animals. Kangaroos and kinkajous, emus and cockatoos roam, fly and even perform for visitors in an attractive setting of gardens and streams. Children will particularly enjoy the parrot show, but the park is fun for all ages. Transport to the park can be provided from the major tourist centres on the island. Just beyond the park is a spectacular mirador from which you can see the cliffs and Isla La Graciosa.

Guinate is about 1km (²/₃ mile) from Rte LZ10, 5km (3 miles) north of Haría. Tel: 928 835 500. Open: daily 10am–5pm. Admission charge (pricey).

The harbour at Orzola

Volcanic caves

When volcanoes erupt, they generate tremendous amounts of heat, molten lava and gases. While the gases usually vent vertically, occasionally they are trapped under a crust of surface lava that cools and hardens before the gases can escape. When this happens, they move horizontally through the mass of lava flowing from the eruption, and create subterranean tunnels and caverns. These caverns and tunnels are sometimes quite close to the surface of the resulting *malpaís*, with only thin brittle coverings of the porous stone. When the roofs of these tunnels and bubbles collapse from erosion, they leave large craters, called *jameos*. In northern Lanzarote you can go into and explore two large *jameos* and the caves formed by the tunnels. These are part of the tunnel system of the volcano Monte Corona, created about 5,000 years ago when the Malpaís de la Corona (the badlands of Corona) were formed.

Cueva de los Verdes

The Jameos de los Verdes are part of a 7km (4¼-mile) volcanic tube that extends from La Corona mountain to – and under – the sea. About 2km (1¼ miles) of it has been opened to visitors, who can walk through it to learn about volcanism and the formation of tubes. The only changes that have been made in the tube are the addition of lights and a paved path to make passage safer. Entry to the cave is through a larger *jameo*, caused when the roof of a bubble chamber collapsed. The tunnel passes through a narrow and low passage before opening out again into larger chambers, some as high as 15m (49ft). The stone of the walls is red, orange and black of iron oxide, calcium carbonate and sulphurous oxide, as well as many other colours, occasionally punctuated with dabs of white. On the return trip you pass to an upper level of the tube where there is a large opening in the floor into another chamber below. The tour takes about an hour.
*26km (16 miles) north of Arrecife.
Tel: 928 848 484. Open: daily
10am–6pm (last tour 6pm).
Admission charge.*

Jameos del Agua

When you combine the ferocity of nature with the genius of an artist you are likely to end up with something spectacular – such as Jameos del Agua. Here César

Manrique, Lanzarote's premier artist, took two *jameos* connected by a cavernous tunnel and created what is both a work of art and a natural wonder. Entry is down a stair into the first *jameo*, called *jameo* Chico, and to a restaurant and bar ingeniously built into the base. From there a path leads into a high vaulted chamber filled with seawater containing a rare species of blind white crabs, usually only found in the blackness of ocean depths. A stone path clings to one side of the tunnel and comes out into a large bar and entertainment area. Stairs lead upwards to another level, still within the *jameo*, where paths and a pool of startling white form a striking contrast with the blackness of the *jameo*. Inside the tunnel is also a huge auditorium created by Manrique, where concerts are frequently held.

27km (17 miles) north of Arrecife. Tel: 928 848 020. Open: daily 9.30am–7pm, Tue, Fri & Sat also 7pm–3am (folkloric shows). Admission charge.

The green of Cueva de los Verdes

Drive: Northern mountains and coast

In an area barely 10km (6 miles) square, the northern tip of Lanzarote combines a 609m (1,998ft) volcanic mountain, an escarpment, white-sand beaches, farmlands and a broad stretch of forbidding black malpaís.

Allow two hours' driving time, without stops.

Begin at Haría.

1 Haría
For descriptions of this town in 'the valley of a thousand palms', see page 68.
Leave Haría on Rte LZ10, heading north. Bear left at the intersection at 1km (²/₃ mile), signposted to Guinate, 3km (1³/₄ miles).

2 Guinate
In the village is a tiny chapel on a lane to the left (visible from the road) and Guinate Tropical Park, where more than 1,300 colourful birds and exotic animals live in a botanic garden. The road ends at a mirador with views similar to those at Mirador del Río.
Return to Rte LZ10 and continue north 1km (²/₃ mile) to Yé.

3 Yé
This mountain town, high on the side of Monte Corona, is another of the island's wine-growing regions. **Bodega Volcán de la Corona** is a low-key, friendly

winery, where you can sample the wines and various liqueurs made from cactus, berries, almonds and honey.
In Yé, turn left at the road signposted to Mirador del Río (2km/1¹/₄ miles).

4 Mirador del Río
César Manrique converted the military battery 450m (1,476ft) above the sea into a mirador, complete with a café (*see p80*).
Return to the main road, and continue around the side of the mountain, to the left turning, signposted to Orzola. Follow this road as it descends to the shore.

5 Orzola
Orzola's harbour, the starting point for boats to Isla La Graciosa, is lined with seafood restaurants (*see pp80–81*).
Turn left onto the coastal road, heading south along the shore.

6 Malpaís de la Corona
The black lava flow from eruptions of Monte Corona formed the coarse black

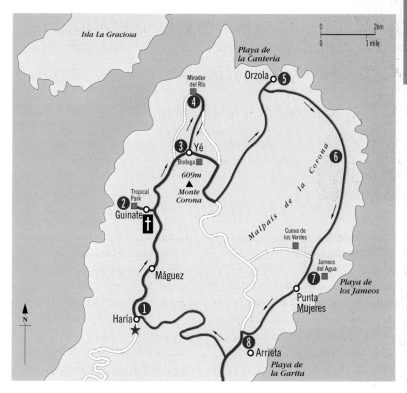

malpaís through which you now travel. Curious areas of white sand dunes are interspersed with the black lava, forming beaches in the coves.
Continue south 9km (5¹/₂ miles) to the entrances for Cueva de los Verdes and Jameos del Agua, directly opposite each other.

7 Cueva de los Verdes and Jameos del Agua

These two major attractions are in the same volcanic tunnel, which extends from Monte Corona to the sea (*see pp82–3*).
Continue south on the coastal road,

past more beaches to Arrieta, 4km (2¹/₂ miles).

8 Arrieta's beaches

The turning for Arrieta is marked by another Manrique 'wind toy' at the roundabout. North of this former fishing village is **Playa de los Jameos**, favoured by surfers and windsurfers. At **Punta Mujeres** are natural pools formed by lava, safe even for small children. South of Arrieta, **Playa de la Garita** is good for surfers.
To return to the starting point at Haría, turn right at Arrieta and follow the road for 6km (3³/₄ miles).

Excursion: Isla La Graciosa

The island of La Graciosa is only 2km (1¹/₄ miles) from Lanzarote, separated from it by a strait called El Río. Its little harbour town of Caleta del Sebo has the few tourist facilities offered here: bicycle hire, a restaurant and a few jeeps that can usually be hired to deliver visitors to the further beaches. Here, also, you will find a few simple pensions and apartments.

What brings people to La Graciosa – apart from the isolation and quiet – is the beaches, and superb surfing and diving. The most spectacular beach is the furthest from town, at about 6km (3³/₄ miles), under one of the island's volcanic mountains. **Playa Las Conchas** offers nearly 0.5km (¹/₃ mile) of white sand. It is dangerous for swimming and very windy, but has beautiful scenery. The closest to town is **Playa Francesca**, about 2km (1¹/₄ miles) southwest of the port; this is the beach most day visitors head for after arriving on the morning boat. The longest beach, **Playa El Salado**, is 1.5km (1 mile) from end to end, and is accessible only by a footpath. Also reached only by foot is **Playa Barranco de los Conejos**, a 3km (1³/₄-mile) walk along the coast.

Because of its open exposure, none of La Graciosa's beaches is safe for swimming. Hip-deep is as far as anyone should enter the water. As in most other parts of the island, beaches are quite windy, so it is wise to carry a sun tent.

La Graciosa's geographic position, at the far north of the Canaries archipelago, places it at the meeting point of the Atlantic and the Mediterranean waters, and directly opposite the Caribbean's tropical currents. A great variety of sea creatures from all three sources mixes here, in waters which never fall below 18°C (64°F) and which are exceedingly clear. All these factors combine to make these some of the finest diving waters in Europe.

Because of its unique marine life, and because the nutrient-rich waters attract sea birds, the entire group of offshore islands here constitutes a marine reserve.

The best way to get around the island is by bicycle. Most of the beaches can be reached this way, although paths and roads are rough. You can bring bicycles to the island on the daily boat or hire them in Caleta del Sebo, where there are repair facilities, too.

Líneas Marítimas Romero runs a 15-minute daily ferry service from Orzola (35km/22 miles north of Arrecife). Reservations tel: 928 401 666.

Departs 10am, noon, 5pm & 6.30pm; returns 8am, 11am, 4pm & 6pm July–Sept, no 6pm or 6.30pm trip Oct–June.

View of La Graciosa from Lanzarote

Fuerteventura

The oldest of the Canary Islands in geological terms, Fuerteventura is perhaps the youngest in terms of tourism. Its origins are volcanic – the central mountains were thrust up from the earth's crust by volcanic eruption 12–17 million years ago. The rest of the island is volcanic lava flow from eruptions two million years ago and a few thousand years ago. It was the latter that left the jagged black malpaís you'll see at Pozo Negro and in the north.

On this apparently barren landscape, farmers have nonetheless managed to grow crops, harvesting enough vegetables to make export possible. This and fishing were the island's mainstay until tourists discovered its long, golden beaches, changing the island's economy and its appearance in the course of a decade.

Tourism is still changing the island's scenery, as new 'towns' spring out of the mountainsides where they drop to the best beaches. Not all of these are well-planned or even attractive, but together they provide lodging for throngs of sunseekers, largely from the UK and Germany. In general, Germans head toward the southern resorts at Costa Calma and Jandía, while Brits are more at home in Caleta de Fuste and Corralejo.

These four areas make up the majority of the tourist development. Of them, Corralejo retains the most character of a Canarian town, with a central area of narrow streets and local businesses. Of the other three, which are 'villages' built entirely for tourists,

Caleta de Fuste is often cited as an example of what these developments should strive to be, with a village centre, well-laid-out streets and low buildings. Plenty of restaurants, from typical Canarian to exotic cuisines, offer a variety of choices to the many self-catering visitors. The southern resorts cater mainly for all-inclusive packages.

The curious traveller will certainly want to hire a car to explore the island's scenic interior, and to sample its beaches and landscapes. Those visiting both Lanzarote and Fuerteventura will find it very quick and easy to cross – with or without a car – on the ferry to Playa Blanca on Lanzarote.

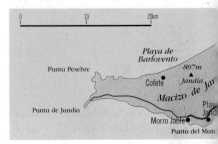

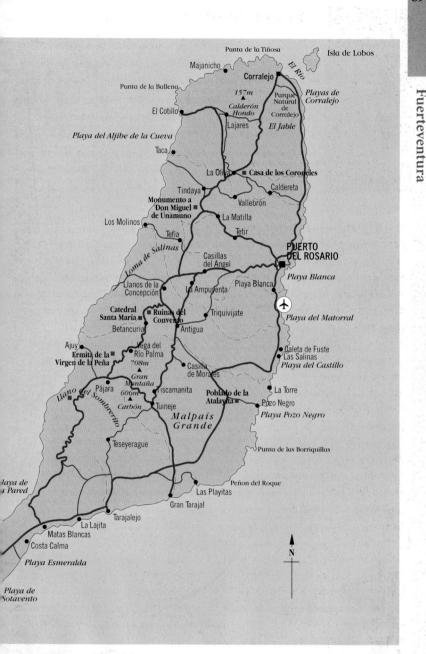

Punta de la Tiñosa

Isla de Lobos

Majanicho

Corralejo

El Río

Punta de la Ballena

Playas de Corralejo

157m
Calderón Hondo

Parque Natural de Corralejo

El Cotillo

Lajares

El Jable

Playa del Aljibe de la Cueva

Taca

La Oliva

Casa de los Coroneles

Tindaya

Caldereta

Monumento a Don Miguel de Unamuno

Vallebrón

Los Molinos

La Matilla

Tefía

Tetir

Loma de Salinas

PUERTO DEL ROSARIO

Casillas del Angel

Playa Blanca

Llanos de la Concepción

La Ampuyenta

Playa Blanca

Catedral Santa María

Ruinas del Convento

Triquivijate

Playa del Matorral

Betancuria

Antigua

Ajuy

Vega del Río Palma

Ermita de la Virgen de la Peña

708m

Caleta de Fuste
Las Salinas
Playa del Castillo

Casilla de Morales

Gran Montaña

Pájara

606m

Tiscamanita

Poblado de la Atalayita

La Torre

Pozo Negro

Carbón

Tuineje

Llano del Sombrerito

Malpaís Grande

Playa Pozo Negro

Teseyerague

Punta de las Borriquillas

Peñon del Roque

laya de a Pared

Las Playitas

Gran Tarajal

Tarajalejo

N

La Lajita

Matas Blancas

Costa Calma

Playa Esmeralda

Playa de Sotavento

Puerto del Rosario

While it's an attractive city with workaday shops and plenty of good restaurants and cafés, the island's capital has little to attract tourists. Ferries leave its harbour for the eight-hour trip to Gran Canaria. The city used to be headquarters for the Spanish Foreign Legion, and their building at the northern end of town is fronted by gardens decorated with artillery. The oldest part of the city, the narrow streets lined with typical Canarian houses, is near the harbour, whose promenade has been renewed with bright tiled benches.

For tourist information in Puerto del Rosario visit the Oficina de Turismo (*Avenida de la Constitución 5. Tel: 928 530 844. Open: Mon–Fri 8am–2pm*). Far more useful is the one at the airport (*Tel: 928 860 604. Open: Mon–Sat 9am–8pm, Sun 11am–4pm*).

Casa de Miguel de Unamuno

The Spanish writer Miguel de Unamuno was exiled to Fuerteventura in 1924 for his opposition to the dictatorial government of the time, and lived at the former Hotel Fuerteventura, opposite the church. His rooms there are preserved as a museum, complete with many of his belongings. Although he was not here by choice, and escaped before his later return to Spain under Franco, he wrote fondly of the island and the kindness of its people, making him something of an adopted native son. A statue of him stands on a mountainside to the north, near Tindaya.

Calle Rosario 11. Tel: 928 851 400. Open: Mon–Fri 9am–1pm, 5–7pm, Sat 9am–1pm. Admission charge.

Centro de Arte Juan Ismael 'Caji'

A 1940s cinema has been converted into a beautiful art centre, which holds contemporary art exhibitions showcasing national and international artists. Just the visit to the building, which is sited right on the beach, is worthwhile.

Calle Almirante Lallermand 30. Tel: 928 859 750. Open: Mon–Sat 10am–1pm & 5–9pm.

Iglesia de la Virgen de Rosario

At the centre of the commercial district, facing the island government building (El Cabildo), the church stands in a small plaza with benches and trees. It is not typical of island architecture, with a rather large square belfry. Beside it, on a bench, sits one of the city's endearing public sculptures, while a kiosk bar stands near the corner of the plaza.

Public sculpture

For a businesslike little city, Puerto del Rosario is quite cultured. In addition to naming its streets after artists, musicians and literary characters (look out for de Falla, Goya, Don Quixote, Dulcinea and Sancho Panza, among others), the city has undertaken an ambitious programme of public sculpture. Some 35 works, ranging from giant seashells along the harbour to large modernist works at major street intersections, span all artistic styles and media, adding interest to a walk around the city. In front of the town hall is a garden inhabited by bronze goats.

Playa Blanca

Close to the city towards the airport is the beach of Playa Blanca, and above it the former parador, now privatised. Although it is not one of the island's best beaches – certainly it cannot compete with the long strands of Jandía or Corralejo – neither is it overdeveloped. The waves are good but there are strong currents, so a flag warning system operates here. The restaurant at Hotel Playa Blanca, the former Parador Nacional, is one of the best in Puerto del Rosario. It's beautifully decadent, with good food and wines.

Tel: 928 851 150. Rte FV2, 3km (1³/₄ miles) south of the city centre.

The waterfront promenade at Puerto del Rosario

Northern Fuerteventura

Corralejo sits almost at the northernmost point of Fuerteventura, and is the landing point for the frequent ferries from Playa Blanca on Lanzarote. It has ample tourism facilities and is adjacent to one of the finest stretches of sand in the Canary Islands. The north coast is popular with surfers and kitesurfers on account of its long, rolling waves and strong, steady winds. Swimming anywhere except in well-protected coves is dangerous.

Isla de Lobos

Isla de Lobos is named after the seals (*lobos marinos*) which used to swim here before they were wiped out in around the 16th century. The island lies just off Corralejo, offering beach, beauty and relative quiet; walkers, birdwatchers and surfers are happy here. Plan a full day to climb to the volcano, where herring gulls and Cory's shearwaters nest, or just follow trails to discover the 100 or so varieties of plants that grow on the island. Watch out, too, for the occasional common stingray and angel shark that appear in the waters. The beach is in a protected lagoon, so it is safe even for children to swim. Take a picnic, or reserve lunch immediately when you land on the island.

In 2009, the Centro de Interpretación de la Isla de Lobos was opened – an exhibition centre about the island's flora, fauna, geology and sealife.

Glass-bottomed boats, built to show off the clear waters en route, and conventional boats depart for the 3km (1³/₄-mile), 15-minute boat trip several times daily, and can be booked at the dock or through your hotel.
Catamaran Celia Cruz. Tel: (639) 140 014. Departs: daily 9.45am.

North Road

The far northern coast of the island is formed of black volcanic rock, broken by coves filled with white sand. Surfers love these remote beaches (although swimming is not safe here) and you can watch them from the road. Be careful as you pull off the road to be sure you are on solid ground, not sand. About halfway between Corralejo and El Cotillo is the little fishing village of Majanicho, from which a road leads off across the Tableros del Guirre to Lajares.

At the far end, where the track meets El Cotillo's coastal road, is the lighthouse, Faro del Tostón. This now houses a museum about the history of fishing on Fuerteventura. The view here is beautiful at sunset, with surfers riding waves highlighted by the setting sun and the sky turning orange behind them. An excellent route for cyclists and walkers, this road may not be suitable for cars beyond Punto de Rincón, just west of the village of Majanicho.

Turn left from Avda. Juan Carlos I in Corralejo, just after the bus station and before the Hesperia Bristol Hotel.

Parque Natural de Corralejo

Southeast of town, past a new tourist suburb of neo-Moorish and ye-olde-Spanish developments, stretches the 10km (6-mile) strand of sand so golden that from neighbouring Lanzarote you can see it gleaming in the afternoon sun. Development ends abruptly at the entrance to Parque Natural de Corralejo, the nature reserve that

The north provides perfect conditions for kitesurfing

protects the beach and dunes. Two large resorts loom incongruously from the sands at the southern end of the reserve, built before environmentalists could gather forces to preserve this wild and beautiful area. With plenty of wide-open space, the beaches are favourites with kitesurfers, but the same stiff breeze they seek makes it wise to bring wind-tents for sunbathing.

Corralejo

Almost overnight the sleepy little port of Corralejo has boomed into a busy resort, with shopping plazas, a theme park and a thoroughly British tone – although still with a Spanish accent. Close to the ferry landing the old town still lies in a maze of streets and

passageways, in the evening filled with touts for the restaurants that crowd the little squares. Further east the main street widens into the new resort, with hotels, shops and more pubs and restaurants. Ferries shuttle cars and passengers back and forth to Lanzarote, a half-hour trip away (*see p184*), and a wide variety of boat excursions and water sports can be booked at kiosks in the harbour (*see pp157–61*).

38km (23 miles) north of the airport. Información Turística at the Muelle Chico, Paseo Marítimo. Tel: 928 860 500 or 928 866 235. Open: Mon–Fri 8am–6.30pm.

Beach and promenade

The ambience of the old fishing town still lingers along the seafront, where the walkway bears little resemblance to the wide palm-lined promenades of purpose-built resorts – and is all the more charming for it. The port end of the beachfront is marked by sculptor Paco Curbelo's 2002 Monumento al Marinero, a striking, larger-than-life bronze depiction of a fisherman's return to his family and, close by, a still-waiting woman. The promenade passes several small sandy areas, a children's playground and a number of restaurants before ending at the main beach. At this wide cove of gold sand, sunloungers, umbrellas and windsurfing equipment are available for hire.

Monumento al Marinero in Corralejo

Baku Water Park

Proving that Corralejo is a 'real' holiday resort, the water park offers

something for almost everyone. Built into the wind-sheltered hillside, eight waterslides range from a short children's chute to 'Kamikaze', and a wave pool creates a variety of different waves. Children's play areas, sunbeds, a whirlpool tub, a café and changing rooms are all within the compound. The swimming pools have waterfalls and slides, and one pool is deep enough for diving.
Avda. de Canarias. Tel: 928 867 227. Open: daily Apr–Oct 10am–6pm. Admission charge.

Flag Beach

Reefs protect both ends of Flag Beach, forming a 400m- (440yd-) long bay, just east of Corralejo, one of the island's prime sites for wind- and kitesurfing.

Winter brings waves and summer brings flat water slalom and freestyle sailing, with the strongest cross-shore winds in the afternoon. Along with offering classes at all levels, the centre sells new and used kites. If you view these as spectator sports only, this is a nice beach to watch from.
Red Shark Kitesurf School, Calle Anzuelo. Tel: 928 867 548. www.redsharkfuerteventura.com. Open: Mon–Sat 10am–1.30pm & 5–9pm.

Market

Above the Baku Water Park complex is a new market area for craftsmen and vendors, replacing the former Monday market nearer the town centre. More local crafts are offered here than in the usual street market, from sand painting

An artist at work depicting Isla de Lobos

and jewellery to wooden wares and aloe-vera skin products.
Avda. de Canarias. Tel: (618) 308 818. Open: Mon & Fri 9am–1pm.

Water sports and excursions

The harbour is the centre for a wide variety of water-based activities, in addition to trips to Isla de Lobos and the ferry to Lanzarote. Passengers for other boats can sign on from hotels and sports shops elsewhere in town, even from stalls in the market. Many of these offer pickups at hotels (*see pp157–9*).

El Cotillo

The urban sprawl of holiday resort development has not yet overtaken the little town of El Cotillo, but signs of its approach are already there. For the present, it is still mostly a cluster of traditional buildings overlooking a pretty harbour and 18th-century stone tower, with a few cafés and restaurants frequented by day-trippers and the surfers who flock to the beaches south of town.
22km (13 1/2 miles) southwest of Corralejo. Tourist information is available in El Tostón (see right).

El Cotillo harbour

The main road into the town ends abruptly at what appears to be only a seawall. But follow the lane downward – or stop and look down – to find quite possibly the prettiest harbour in the Canary Islands. Colourful little fishing boats and dinghies bob in a

pool surrounded by low black cliffs with a craggy outcrop of rock almost enclosing one end. More boats are pulled up on the launch ramp. Behind and above is the round stone tower of El Tostón and a couple of cafés, and behind them rises the shoulder of a volcano. Photographers should note that the sun illuminates this scene with the best light in the afternoon. Another tiny cove just to the north is the older harbour, with more cafés spilling onto the pavement, next to an attractive sculpture of fishermen with a boat.

El Tostón

Built in 1743 to fend off English pirates, the Castillo de Rico Roque, better known as El Tostón or Fortaleza del Tostón, sits above the harbour near the centre of El Cotillo. Like the round forts at Caleta de Fuste and Playa Blanca, its tapering walls have no door at ground level, and the only access is up a narrow exterior stair to a single door set high in the wall. The fort has been restored and serves as a tourist information point. It also has a gallery of changing exhibits, although it does not always keep to its posted hours.
Open: Mon–Fri 9am–4pm, Sat & Sun 9am–3pm.

Faro del Tostón and beaches

Just north of the town, on the way to the candy-striped Tostón lighthouse (*faro*), are several little coves where fine white sand fills the hollows between rough black lava rocks, a visually beautiful combination bordering the very blue sea. Except in completely protected rock coves, swimming is very dangerous off this coast, with strong winds and currents to sweep the unwary out to sea. Camping and caravanning are allowed – or at least tolerated – at some of these. But the most surprising feature is the architecture of the holiday homes that are scattered along this shore. Many are in a charming modern interpretation of Art Nouveau, with curving lines and quirky architectural adornments. Those available as self-catering accommodation have small signs showing their telephone numbers.

Playa del Aljibe de la Cueva

South of El Cotillo, an unpaved track follows the coast atop the cliffs. To find the beaches below, look for groups of parked vehicles and follow the even smaller tracks to join them. Views from the headlands are wonderful, best in the afternoon light. At the foot of the cliffs are golden-sand beaches favoured by surfers. Near El Tostón is Holly Land, an art installation of surfboard-shaped reflective panels.

Playa Los Lagos

The best beach in the north to visit with children, this is a series of little shell-like white sand bays. It is great for swimmers and has a couple of beach restaurants nearby, such as the beach shack 'Torino' where they serve the catch of the day and beautiful paella.

Pastelería El Goloso is a glorious French bakery, perfect for a tea stop, selling cakes, baguettes and fresh juices.
Pecho Saavecha 1. Tel: 928 538 668.

Wonderful beaches are found near El Cotillo

Lajares

The small inland town of Lajares was a centre for agriculture, despite its location in the middle of the Malpaís de la Arena, an ancient lava flow. In a little settlement in the southern part of the village (turn just past the Lucha Canaria stadium), next to the trim little church, are two windmills in good repair, until fairly recently in use to grind the locals' grain. Lajares has long been known for its fine needlework, and a school of embroidery has operated here for more than half a century.

The volcano of Calderón Hondo lies north of town, along with Montaña Colorada. An ancient trail passes through Lajares, a portion of which has been restored to provide walkers with access to the volcano (*see pp106–7*). *Lajares is 11km (7 miles) southwest of Corralejo and 7km (4¹/₄ miles) east of El Cotillo.*

Cueva del Llano

The cave was formed by a lava flow that hardened on the top and continued to evolve, acting as a natural drain and creating fossils as trapped sediment hardened into stone. Tours are conducted by trained naturalists who show how the lava tubes were formed and explain the geological history of the island and the cave. Visitors, who wear miners' helmets for light, see signs of the cave's primitive inhabitants, the Makos, and learn about the blind albino spiders that live deep in the cave. Even if you tour Cueva de los Verdes on Lanzarote, this cave is an entirely different – and fascinating – experience, and the tour is more educational.
Open: Tue–Sat 10am–6pm, tours every half hour. Admission charge.

Escuela de Artesanía Canaria Sra Hernández

Although you may see demonstrations elsewhere of the intricate pulled-thread embroidery for which the islands are so well known, this is an active school where the art is taught and practised regularly. There will almost certainly be someone working, and there will be works in progress on the frames, so you

Casas de Arribas church in Lajares

can see how it is done. The studio offers an excellent selection of handmade needlework, from handkerchiefs and napkins to entire sets of table linen. Everything here is handmade locally, with none of the imports often found in shops and markets.

Plaza Santa María, Lajares. Tel: 928 868 300. Open: Mon–Fri 9am–7pm, Sat 9am–3pm. Free admission.

Lucha Canaria

Lajares is a centre for the uniquely Canarian form of wrestling, Lucha Canaria. The stadium is not an attraction in its own right, but there you will see posters announcing the next matches. This sport, played by teams of wrestlers who compete in a series of individual contests, draws a partisan crowd of locals who will welcome you to cheer for their home team. Those familiar with Cumberland or Westmoreland wrestling will recognise Lucha Canaria as a similar form of the sport.

Rte FV109, in the village centre.

La Oliva

During the 1700s, this village shared the seat of government with Antigua, and it later became a capital on its own. This former importance is evident in its buildings: the grand Casa de los

The Cueva del Llano offers an insight into Fuerteventura's geological history

The imposing Casa de los Coroneles

Coroneles and the parish church, Nuestra Señora de la Candelaria. Although the Casa de los Coroneles has been restored, another once-grand home of the priests, **Casa del Inglés**, with its finely carved wooden embellishments, is falling into decay, its formerly beautiful balcony hanging precariously.

Like many Fuerteventura towns, La Oliva is a curious blend of new and freshly whitewashed buildings mixed with ruins of crumbling stone and stucco.

La Oliva is 16km (10 miles) south of Corralejo.

Casa de los Coroneles

The House of the Colonels, a 40-room mansion built by the Colonels who virtually ruled the island in the early 1700s, fell on hard times after Franco's army left it in the mid-20th century. Originally the showpiece of the island, its grandeur was so astonishing compared to the meagre peasants' homes around it that local people described it in ironic hyperbole. Even today you will hear tour guides insist that the house has as many windows and doors as there are days in a year. Recent restoration has made it once again the showplace of the island, with magnificent wooden doors, deep panelled windows and intricately carved balconies. Go out onto the upper terrace, then to the tower for views over the tiled roofs to the volcano beyond.

Over the door is a crest with designs of a crown with a tree and a goat.
At the eastern side of town, signposted from the church. Open: Tue–Sun 10am–2pm & 4.30–7pm. Free admission.

Casa de la Cilla

The harvesting of grain, once an important product of the island's farms, is explored from the field to the mill in this small museum. Tools, old photographs and attractive displays chronicle the story.
West of the church, La Oliva. Tel: 928 851 400. Open: Tue–Fri & Sun 9.30am–5.30pm. Admission charge.

Nuestra Señora de la Candelaria

The dark stone tower and buttressed walls of the church, built in 1717, form a building larger than most churches on the island. Behind its nicely carved wooden doors, the inside is richly endowed, too, with a *mudéjar* ceiling, a baroque painting at the altar by Juan de Miranda and good trompe l'œil decoration, not commonly seen here. One of the island's most interesting churches, it also features a delicate wooden pulpit, formerly painted, which is supported on an impossibly fragile pedestal, only 15cm (6in) in diameter at its narrowest.

La Oliva environs

Just to the north of La Oliva, so close that they seem to blend together, is Villaverde. Again, with characteristic hyperbole, islanders facetiously call this town 'Little Hollywood' after the foreigners who have built or restored houses here. To the south, between two mountains, is Tindaya, known for its holy mountain covered in aboriginal engravings.

La Rosita

The attractive farm of La Rosita has been preserved by the family that has farmed here for generations, as an example of traditional farming. Camels are still used here to demonstrate their

Entrance to La Rosita

place in traditional island farming, pulling ploughs and doing other farm work. The camels are also used to give visitors rides through the farm's fields and gardens, where they will see how the volcanic soil can produce crops. Children will enjoy the farm animals, as well as a few more exotic ones. In the small museum and outbuildings are implements used in cheesemaking and other activities, as well as photographs of the region to show what farm life was like in the past. This family farm is a nice contrast – and complement – to the museum village of La Alcogida (*see pp103–4*), and together they give a good picture of island life as it was before tourism.
Rte FV101, north of Villaverde, 3km (1³/₄ miles) south of the FV109 intersection. Open: Mon–Sat 10am–6pm. Admission charge.

Monumento a Don Miguel de Unamuno

On the dark and beautiful volcano called Montaña Quemada stands an almost austere monument to the island's adopted native son, the writer Miguel de Unamuno. Exiled here in 1924 for his outspoken opposition to the dictatorial government in Madrid, he wrote appreciatively of the island while here and throughout his career, endearing himself to its residents even today. The tall, gaunt likeness stands on a plain plinth against the stark, barren landscapes he described. The mountain where it stands, the 294m (965ft)

Montaña Quemada, is an almost symmetrical volcanic cone.
Rte FV10, south of Tindaya.

Tindaya

Although the town is small, its church has more than its share of art, with a good baroque altar, paintings and a statue of the **Virgen de la Caridad**. The town has long been a centre for the Majorero goats' cheeses that Fuerteventura is known for (*see pp108–9*). **Hijos de Vera Montelongo** is easy to spot on the hillside and you can visit this cheesemaker to buy wheels of fresh, aged or smoked goats' cheese and peek through the large glass windows of the office to see it being made.
Tel: 928 865 509. Open: Mon–Sat 8.30am–2pm.

Montaña Tindaya

At 401m (1,316ft) high, the mountain of Tindaya stands alone in the flat landscape. Considered by the island's native population to be a sacred place, the summit of the mountain is marked by strange podomorphs. These are outsized footprint designs carved into its rock surfaces. They all point towards the island of Tenerife, whose tallest mountain, Teide – also the tallest mountain in Spain – is visible from Tindaya's summit on clear days. It is thought that aboriginals associated the smoke and fire issuing from Teide's active crater with the devil, or some other source of evil, and that these footprints were protective symbols. You will find that trails to the summit are not marked as government permission is required to climb the mountain because of its archaeological importance.

Tefía and La Alcogida

The village of Tefía is quite small, and its primary interest to the traveller is a group of small farms just to its south, which have been restored as a museum village. This is also the turn-off point for the fishing village of Los Molinos.

Ecomuseo de La Alcogida

The little settlement of seven farms just outside of Tefía was almost a ghost village until the entire assemblage was restored as a museum. It provides an excellent chance to see inside typical Canarian homes, and to get a sense of how people in various economic circumstances lived throughout much

The landscape between La Oliva and Villaverde

of the 20th century. The arrangement is much the same in all these household complexes, with individual rooms leading off a central open patio. The first house is now the entrance building, with a small café and a craft shop. The second shows how a very modest family lived; note the interesting cane ceiling. The third has been converted into an exhibition space, with an excellent display on Canarian pulled-thread work. Various patterns had names, much in the same way that early American quilt patterns were named: star-of-the-sea, etc. The fourth, the home of a well-to-do family, is especially interesting for

its kitchen, with a built-in hearth/stove and oven. The last houses are given to craft workers' workshops, in many of which there are demonstrations. Here you might watch Canarian pulled-thread embroidery, tin working, basketry, weaving, leatherwork, pottery or stone cutting in progress.

Rte FV207, just south of Tefía.
Tel: 928 175 343. Open: Tue–Fri &
Sun 9.30am–5.30pm. Admission charge.

Los Molinos

Directly west of Tefía, a paved road follows along the edge of a rocky canyon, Barranco de Los Molinos, to the village of Los Molinos, tucked into a narrow cove between two steep headlands of black-and-white-striped cliffs. To reach the village, you must park the car and walk across a little footbridge, where ducks hope you will remember to bring them a bread roll from your lunch. Along with two popular restaurants, the town has an interesting small shrine at the landing where fishing boats are hauled ashore. Inside, the altar is decorated with seashells, coral and sea horses.

Windmills

Within sight of La Alcogida are two restored windmills, of different types. The older of the two is a round stone mill atop a hill directly behind the museum, on the grounds of a crafts school operated by the museum. The

The farm museum at La Alcogida

second, which is open more frequently, is a wooden mill on the roof of a small building, a style that became common later on. You can go inside the building to see the inner workings and climb up to the roof to inspect the sails and structure. This is a working mill, and they sell *gofio* ground there.

Rte FV207, at the southern end of Tefía. Free admission.

Stone windmill near La Alcogida

Walk: El Sendero de Bayuyo

This walk follows an ancient pathway (sendero), recently improved by the island tourism authorities to show something of the volcanic origins and wild landscape of Fuerteventura. It is an easy walk, suitable for all ages and levels of fitness, and if you can time the walk for sunset you will enjoy the wonderful sight of the landscape bathed in rich velvety reds, browns and purples. Out of the sun, you may need to wrap up (particularly in winter).

For El Sendero de Bayuyo, turn off the Lajares road by the Campo de Fútbol at the eastern end of town. Exactly 1km (²/₃ mile) down the road, the path is marked, on the right.

For this walk you need to allow 1½ hours. Remember that darkness falls quickly at this latitude, so if you want to see the sunset you need to allow enough time to return and do carry torches.

The walk initially heads straight for Montaña Colorada (Coloured Mountain), an ancient volcano of many hues, then skirts round it to the right. At this point, the path appears to start climbing the mountain ahead, but if you look to the right you will see the stone-lined path carrying on around the base. Notice the low stone walls dividing the fields; even in this wilderness, crops are grown.

Ancient volcanoes formed the Fuerteventura landscape

Once around Montaña Colorada, the path climbs slowly, spiralling up a second volcano, Calderón Hondo. The views backwards (south), to the side (east), and forwards (north) sweep across empty countryside, bordered by ancient, softly rounded volcanic cones. After 20 minutes you will see the beach of Corralejo ahead in the distance. After a few minutes, the Isla de Lobos (right) and Lanzarote (in the far distance) become clear.

Take the fork to the left. After about 30 minutes, the path ascends to the top of Calderón y Hondo.

Here, 223m (732ft) above Corralejo, there is a viewing platform (and safety rails) for looking down into the 8,000-year-old crater. The golden beaches of Playa Blanca and volcanic landscape of Lanzarote are also clearly visible.

A VOLCANIC EXTENSION

The path of Bayuyo is part of an old trail which connects Corralejo to the interior. This land was created some 8,000 years ago in a series of volcanic eruptions which formed the present northern coast of the island, and also threw up the island of Los Lobos. To continue to Corralejo, take the path leading down to the sea, visible from Calderón Hondo. The last volcano before Corralejo is Bayuyo, the highest of the group. It's an easy climb, and offers the best views north. Allow three hours' walking to get to Corralejo.

A short taxi ride (about 10km/6 miles) will get you back to the start of the route.

Descend the path and continue down to the left. Disappointingly, the path ends in a small, scrubby, sandy area. If you have proper walking gear and are feeling adventurous, you can walk right round the base of the volcanoes. If not, simply return along the same path.

Walk: El Sendero de Bayuyo

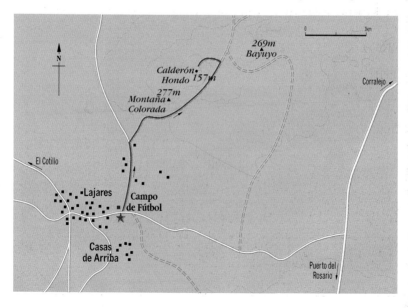

Fuerteventura's own:
Majorero cheese

Only one goats' cheese in the whole of Spain has been judged so fine that it has been granted its own *denominación de origen* (DOC) label, an honour reserved for only the very best food and wine products. It is from Fuerteventura, and the cheese is called Majorero – the islanders' name for all past and present residents of the island.

Once a primary feature of island scenery, goats had declined in population over many years – until recently. Rising again in popularity, these animals can again be seen everywhere, grazing on the apparently barren hillsides. Especially near Morro Jable in the south of the island, goatherds and their dogs can be seen on the moor with their flocks. Goats being herded between their farms and the moor are not an uncommon sight on the roads. Although goat meat is on many

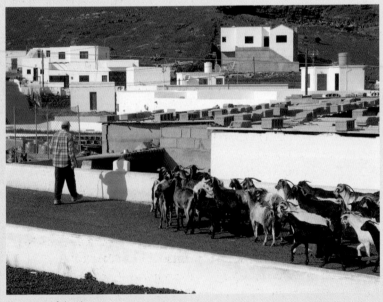

The source of the cheese

The finished article

islands' menus, the more popular use for these goats is for the production of cheese.

When young, the cheese is crumbly and has a white powdery rind, but as it ages the rind turns yellow and the cheese becomes firmer. It is delicious either way, and no trip to Fuerteventura is complete without sampling it. Look for it on menus (if you don't see it, ask), or buy some at cheesemakers and in grocery stores. As you travel, especially in the northern part of the island, you may see signs for cheesemakers on inland roadsides.

The area around Tindaya is especially known as a centre for cheesemaking. In the town itself, it is easy to spot **Hijos de Vera Montelongo** by the large sign and logo on the side of the building, on the hillside above the highway. When it is being made, visitors can peek through the window in the office to watch the process, and they can buy wheels of fresh, aged or smoked goats' cheese from the cooler. *Tindaya. Tel: 928 865 509.*
Open: Mon–Sat 8.30am–2pm.

Quesos de Guríamen have won the Best Spanish Goats' Cheese award three times. It is produced in Villaverde at their **Fábrica de Quesos Guríamen** (*Calle Las Huertas (behind Impescasa supermarket). Tel: 617 578 731/648 075 168. quesosguiriamen@hotmail.com*).

Montelango Gourmet specialises in locally produced fine foods, including cheeses from Tindaya (*Calle Salamanca 12, Puerto del Rosario. Tel: 928 855 480. Open: Mon–Fri 10am–2pm & 5–8pm, Sat 9am–1pm*).

Central Fuerteventura

While the stunning beaches of Fuerteventura's north and south shores draw the sun-worshippers, its centre draws those who want to know something of its history and local culture. Here are two of its early capitals, a revered shrine and other historic churches. The central part of the island is not without its own beaches and resorts, with an excellent example of a 'made-for-tourists' town at Caleta de Fuste.

Antigua

Founded in the late 15th century, Antigua was the island's capital briefly in the early 1800s. It is a very attractive town, with its large, graceful church sitting at the head of a wide, tree-shaded plaza. Standing apart from the cubic white houses is **La Casa del Porton**, an 18th-century manor house.

The **Feria Insular de Artesanía**, held in early May or early June each year, is a major folk festival, with traditional craftspeople demonstrating and selling their wares and the local folkloric music and dance group performing. Befitting its status as one of the oldest towns on the island, Antigua is a centre for traditional arts, with an active local folk-life group.

Molino de Antigua (Windmill)

The name does not begin to suggest the variety of attractions gathered in this complex just north of Antigua. Along with the restored round windmill with its four sails is a round stone granary,

a museum of archaeology, an excellent craft shop and a nicely designed cactus garden – any one of which would be well worth the very low entrance fee. You can climb to the top of the windmill to see the great wooden cogs that operate the grinding mill below. Displays in the museum chronicle the finds at Villaverde and barranco Butihondo, where a volcanic tube was occupied from as early as the 3rd century. Artefacts include pottery, shell ornaments and primitive tools.

In the *Artesanía* are displays of traditional crafts, and one of the finest selections of handicrafts anywhere in the Canary Islands. Along with the expected pulled-thread embroidery are woven palm baskets and hats, terracotta pottery based on designs of the prehistoric inhabitants, excellent wood carving, hand weaving, tin work, painted silk scarves, silver jewellery and work in other media. Motifs and techniques range from those of the oldest island crafts to stunning modern designs.

The old round building that used to store grain has been restored and adapted as a restaurant and café. The design is the work of the artist César Manrique, whose work is seen all over Lanzarote, but less frequently on this neighbouring island. The original architecture is still quite evident, and the interior has been left to show its structural detail. Visitors are welcome to go inside to see the building, even if they do not plan to have a meal there. The café serves traditional local teacakes. *Rte FV20, north of Antigua. Tel: 928 878 041. Open: Tue–Fri & Sun 9.30am–5.30pm. Admission charge.*

Nuestra Señora de Antigua

Built in the traditional island style, with its corners and doorways outlined in dark native stone, Antigua's church is one of the oldest on Fuerteventura, as well as one of the prettiest and most interesting. It was built in 1785 and restored in the 19th century. Inside (it's open more frequently than the little village churches) is a naïve painting of the Judgement Day on a side wall, a pink-and-green-painted main altar and painted side altars. There is a good wooden ceiling in the chancel and the pulpit has a painted canopy.

Inside Nuestra Señora de Antigua

Windmills

The wind is ever-present in Lanzarote and Fuerteventura, sweeping off the North African land mass, sometimes bringing Saharan sand and the occasional locust with it. That the wind has long served utilitarian purposes is clear from the number of windmills that pepper the landscapes of both islands. Capturing the wind was an important adjunct to farming, and its most important use was to grind grains. Near farming communities you will still see the round bodies of tower mills, many of them in various states of restoration. These are the oldest, reminiscent of the mills of La Mancha, but usually one storey taller. While many of these are now derelict, a number have been restored and some of them are still used to grind the corn, barley and other grains that are used in traditional Canarian dishes. Look for the three-storey white towers with four sails in front and a large pole angled from the rear. The pole allows the miller to turn the top of the mill to catch advantageous winds.

Look out also for trestle tower mills, tall (about 6m/20ft) wooden towers raised on top of low, flat buildings. The towers are open wooden work, usually with four sails. Only the top platform is rigged to turn into the wind. The power of the wind is transmitted down a metal shaft to grind wheels located in the building below. These mills, also used for grinding grains, came later – in the late 1800s. Interestingly, Canarians have different names for these mills. The sturdy, round, stone-built ones are called *molinos*, while the more delicate trestle mills are called *molinas*.

Where there is agriculture there is also a need for water, and the wind has also been harnessed to provide that resource. More modern tall metal towers of water pumps stand out in fields and amid farm buildings. While many are in poor repair, a good number are well maintained and still fulfil their original purpose. These windmills were first introduced to Fuerteventura by an emigrant who returned to the island from Cuba.

The newest use of the wind that sweeps the islands is in producing electricity. In addition to scattered individual generators, a major power station is located in the northern mountains at Parque Eólico (Lanzarote), where 38 of the newest wind turbines produce electricity for the island.

La Rosita, in the north of Fuerteventura

Where to find them: One of the best places to see a tower grist mill on Lanzarote is the Museo Agrícola El Patio at Tiagua. There is also a wooden tower mill at the museum. Both buildings and their machinery have been restored. Another is open at Jardín de Cactus in Guatiza. On Fuerteventura, Molino de Antigua is built around a restored and operating tower mill. The farm museum of La Alcogida at Tefía has a restored tower mill on a hill behind it and a wooden tower mill directly adjacent to the road, just at the end of the village. Fuerteventura also has the outstanding Windmill Interpretive Centre at Tiscamanita, which has the best explanation of man's use of the wind. Parque Eólico, with its wind turbines, is off Rte LZ10, north of Teguise.

Betancuria

Betancuria's history is akin to that of Teguise on Lanzarote. Its founder, the island's conqueror Jean de Béthencourt, chose this inland site for his capital in 1405 to escape pirate attacks. Its valley location was also fertile and had a comparatively high water table. But like the pirates that attacked Teguise, the marauders were undeterred, and in 1593 destroyed the church and shipped off 600 Christians to slavery.

Betancuria continued to be the island's capital until 1834, and still retains its air of a gracious colonial capital, albeit a very small one. Some of its houses date back more than five centuries.

31km (19 miles) southwest of Puerto del Rosario.

Calle Jean de Béthencourt

Betancuria lies in layers up the sides of a valley, through which once flowed a year-round river, and its streets reflect the irregular topography. The main square, Plaza Santa María, is carved into the hillside and approached by steps from above. Along the top of the wall at the uphill side runs Calle Jean de Béthencourt, a narrow, pretty street, lined by small houses with picturesque doorways. A carved wooden balcony overhangs the street, and its northern end is punctuated by the church tower.

Casa Santa María

Restored and adapted for use as a restaurant and café, the house across the plaza from the church is worth looking into for its fine carved wooden ceilings. Such ceilings are usually seen only in church chancels. The building is in typical Canarian style, built around enclosed central courtyards.

Plaza de Santa María. Tel: 928 878 282. Open: July–Aug Mon–Sat noon–7pm, Sept–June Mon–Sat 11am–6pm.

Cathedral: Santa María de Betancuria

Rebuilt in 1691 after its destruction by pirates a century earlier, the church retains only parts of the columns and bell tower of the original building. Its entrance, at the side of the building facing onto the plaza, has beautiful carved wooden doors framed in carved stone, whose terracotta colour matches the quoins of the bell tower. The plain interior has naïve-style painted side altars and a baroque high altar embellished in gold. In a side aisle is a Judgement Day painting.

Plaza de Santa María. Open: Mon–Sat 10am–5pm. Opening times may alternate between the church and Museo de Arte Sacro, changing on each half hour and lasting for half an hour. Admission charge (includes Museo de Arte Sacro).

Centro de Artesanía

A wide range of traditional crafts is displayed, sold and demonstrated in the *Artesanía*, next to Casa Santa María; demonstrations may include pottery, weaving, basketry, pulled-thread work, bread baking in a wood oven, and possibly traditional musical instruments. *Plaza Santa María. Open: Mon–Sat 11am–4pm.*

Mirador Morro Velosa
Near the summit of one of the mountains north of Betancuria is a viewpoint with a restaurant. The building, designed by Lanzarote artist César Manrique, provides a sheltered setting for enjoying the views in every direction. If the gateway is closed, at the base of its road is a good view down into Betancuria's valley, and just to the

The entrance to Santa María de Betancuria

south, on FV30, is another mirador. This one has views from either side of the road, with signs identifying the mountains and towns visible in each direction. The view to the north encompasses the long valley and the town of Valle de Santa Inés, and to the south, beyond Betancuria, is one of the island's tallest mountains.
Rte FV30, 2km (1¹/₄ miles) north of Betancuria.

Museo Arqueológico

A traditional house has been adapted as a museum, combining examples of domestic life with displays on local archaeology and palaeontology. Accounts of the first European experiences on the island are combined with artefacts from the Mahos, pre-Hispanic inhabitants. This world of aboriginal people is further explored through religious objects and a large collection of pottery, and among the most interesting of these artefacts is a frieze recovered from the caves of Villaverde, showing a row of human figures. Palaeontology exhibits show the geology of the island, and include fossils as well as bones from archaeological digs in Villaverde. A printed English-language guide to the prehistory exhibits is available at the entrance.
Calle Roberto Roldán. Tel: 928 878 241. Open: Tue–Sat 10am–5pm. Admission charge.

Museo de Arte Sacro

The former presbytery close to the church houses art from the church's own treasury and from the Convent of

The view to the north of Mirador Morro Velosa

Ruins of the Franciscan convent

San Buenaventura, closed for more than half a century and now in partial ruin. The most important treasures housed here are a figure of Santiago and the Pendón de la Conquista. The former shows Santiago, St James, in his role as Moor-slayer, and such images were brought here during the Christian conquest in hopes of subduing – and thus converting – the local inhabitants. The Pendón, the Banner of the Conquest, is a flag which the islanders believe to be the original carried by Béthencourt upon his arrival on the island.

Calle Plaza Santa María. Open: Mon–Sat 10am–5pm. Opening times alternate between the church & museum, changing on each half hour & lasting *for half an hour. Admission charge (includes church).*

Ruinas del Convento San Buenaventura
Visible below the road entering town from the north, or a 5-minute walk from the town centre, the Franciscan Convent of San Buenaventura was built in 1414, shortly after the arrival of the Norman conquerors. After the convent was closed in the 1930s, the roof was removed and sold to pay for grain and water during a severe drought. Today the convent stands roofless and abandoned, although in this climate, where rain is not common, it is still in good condition. The art from the convent is in the Museo de Arte Sacro (*see opposite*).

Diving lessons at Barcelo Club el Castillo

Caleta de Fuste

Although it is a new town, built exclusively for tourism, Caleta de Fuste avoids much of the artificial feel of other such creations. It is considered the most successful of its type, with a mix of restaurants, lodgings, shops and businesses, along with holiday activities. Confusingly, some older publications and maps may refer to this town as El Castillo, and the entire coast along here (although less frequently) as Costa Caleta. A market (*Sat 9am–1pm*) offers no local crafts; some Moroccan leatherwork is nice, but most offerings are cheap imports.

11km (7 miles) south of the airport. Información Turismo, Alcalde Juan Ramón 10. Tel: 928 163 286. Open: (winter) Mon–Sat 9am–2pm, (summer) Mon–Sat 9am–1pm.

Beaches and water sports

The sandy beach inside the cove at Caleta de Fuste is man-made, and protected by a breakwater. Its gently sloping sand makes a long area of shallow water safe for children, and sunbeds and umbrellas are available. It is one of the few enclosed beaches where swimmers are safe from the Atlantic currents. At the marina adjoining the beach at the far end a variety of watersports is on offer, with equipment available for hire. A windsurfing school and dive centre also operate here (*see pp158 and 161*).

Castillo de Fuste

Inside the grounds of Barcelo Club el Castillo, at the marina, is Castillo de Fuste. This round tower, much larger than the one at El Cotillo, dates from the mid-1700s, when the island was subject to attack by English pirates. Like the others of that era, its entrance sits high and is accessed over a drawbridge at the top of a set of stairs. The setting for this rather forbidding black fort is incongruous, to say the least, surrounded by gardens, bright blue swimming pools and children's splash pools. The public is welcome to wander around.

Oceanarium Explorer

An up-close encounter with local sea life, plus a visit from an 'exotic' Californian sea lion named Harley, are part of the experiences offered in two separate boat trips at this marine centre. The glass-bottomed 'submarine' has a deep transparent hull which allows passengers to look through the unusually clear waters and see fish, octopus, stingrays and sharks. A longer sail on a catamaran goes south along the shore to see the turtles off Pozo Negro and to swim or snorkel among the fish that inhabit the reef. Each trip includes a nature guide and a tour of the small oceanarium, where visitors can touch most of the creatures. And both tours include a visit with Harley, who performs in the open sea.

Puerto Castillo yacht harbour. Tel: 928 163 514. Open: daily sailings 10.30am–4.30pm. Admission charge.

Paseo Marítimo Promenade

A wide paved promenade extends from the Puerto Castillo yacht harbour, near the Castillo, along the rocky shore in front of the hotel complexes and beyond to Costa de Antigua, about 1km (^{2}/$_3$ mile) to the north. In front of Elba Castillo de Antigua, after the promenade turns towards the sea, look back at the black rocks and surf at the point (in front of the space between the two hotel buildings) to see the cauldron in the rocky shore; when waves hit just right, spray shoots up into the cauldron as though it were boiling.

Las Salinas

Although surrounded by saltwater, salt was a valuable commodity for Fuerteventura in the days when the island's livelihood depended on fishing. Fish were preserved by salting, and thus could be shipped to markets all over Europe and South America. The only

The harbour at Caleta de Fuste

surviving saltpan on Fuerteventura is at Las Salinas. There's not much more to the town, except a few houses and a little seafood restaurant that will pick up guests from their Caleta de Fuste hotels. To its south, a Parque Natural protects a region of sharp ridges that ends in a rocky coastline.
Rte FV2, 3km (1³/₄ miles) south of Caleta de Fuste.

Museo de Sal

Examining salt – its sources, extraction, uses and importance in history – is the purpose of the museum overlooking the well-preserved working saltpans. Although few actual artefacts are shown, the exhibits are interesting, and an excellent brochure translates their text into English. Outside, the saltpans are open so that visitors can walk along the walls and see how they work. The pans consist of a grid of wide pools enclosed by low walls, meticulously constructed of small black cobbles. Signs explain the process of admitting seawater at the high tide, and allowing just enough to gather for evaporation.
Salinas del Carmen. Tel: 928 174 926. Open: Tue–Sat 10am–6pm. Admission charge.

Whale

While the saltpans are unusual and interesting to visit, the sight awaiting visitors along the shore is more surprising. There, elevated on a supporting framework, is the complete skeleton of a whale. The creature was found on the beach at the northern part of the island; a fishing net wrapped around its mouth had caused it to die of starvation.

Pozo Negro

Beyond the series of ochre-coloured ridges and ravines south of Las Salinas, a road leads along a valley floor towards the sea. Shortly after the turning, past a large agricultural experiment station of covered fields, is a lay-by. Below, a river of black lava seems to have been frozen in mid-flow, contrasting sharply with the reddish-tan of the surrounding mountainsides. The jagged sea of crumbled lava – a *malpaís* – is so clearly defined that you can see the exact path the lava followed as it flowed to the sea. At the end is the little fishing village of Pozo Negro, with a youth hostel, rudimentary campsite and a black-sand beach in a cove between two tall headlands.
The turn from Rte FV2 is 18km (11 miles) south of Caleta de Fuste.

Las Salinas Reef dive sites

The reefs along the shore south of Caleta de Fuste offer extraordinary dive waters, at a variety of depths suitable for all levels of skill. Among these are the Salinas El Tazor Reef, 12–35m (39–115ft) deep with tremendous fish activity, including schools of barracuda. In the crevices and grottoes of Castillo Baranca Reef are several varieties of moray eel, including polka-dot and tiger. The

Salinas-Tesoro Negro Reef has walls of black coral, with sponges and anemones.

Poblado de la Atalayita

The newly opened interpretation centre chronicles the history of the Berber peoples who, in the first millennium BC, built and inhabited the substantial village whose ruins you can explore. The descriptive map (in English) shows the several layers of habitation here, and leads also to a small volcanic cone you can climb for views over the village and the sea.

FV420, Pozo Negro. Open: Tue–Sat 10am–6pm. Free admission.

The whale skeleton at Las Salinas

Pájara and Tuineje

The attractive town of Pájara is positively leafy, with gardens lining the riverbank and spilling over into green patches along the main street. A wide walkway leads from the central intersection, where there is a good *artesanía* with local crafts, past the carved doors of the village church and across the river to a plantation of palms. Another tree-lined promenade follows the stream to a garden and a monument in red stone showing a farmer milking a goat. This green interlude is a surprising contrast to the otherwise stark landscapes of the island.

15km (9¹/₂ miles) south of Betancuria.

Camel-driven pump

Opposite the door of Nuestra Señora de la Regla is a sight that was once common on the island, but is now quite rare – a camel-driven bucket pump. Water was pulled from the earth by the camel walking round the circular enclosure.

Nuestra Señora de la Regla

In the centre of the village, surrounded by trees, is the church, unique on the island in several respects. Dating from 1645–87, the church is best known for its red sandstone doorway, carved in designs reminiscent of Aztec motifs representing suns and snakes, lions and

Statue of a farmer in Pájara

doves. The origin of the portal is a mystery, and the church is just as unusual inside. It has two naves, each with a baroque high altar of gilded polychrome. The image of the Virgin standing in a deep alcove was brought to the island by a wealthy emigrant. Notice the fine carved ceiling in the left altar. To the right of the entrance is a coin box for illuminating the altars. *Open: 11am–1pm & 5–7pm.*

San Miguel Arcangel

Near Tuineje, in 1740, a band of 50 English pirates alighted from their ships with guns and cannon, bent on their usual pirate activities. To their surprise, they were met by a determined band of local farmers, armed with five pistols and an assortment of farm tools. The farm tools proved the most useful, for with these the farmers were able to attack while the pirates were reloading. Along with killing 30 of the pirates, the farmers captured their cannon (on display at the museum in Betancuria), with a loss of only five local lives. The battle is recorded in two paintings in the church of San Miguel Arcangel in Tuineje. Built 50 years after the battle, the church has a baroque high altar with paintings of St Michael and Our Lady of Good Health, in the lower section of the altar.

Windmill Interpretive Centre

Although other museums on the islands have windmills, this one deserves a visit for its excellent explanation of how the

The Windmill Interpretive Centre at Tiscamanita

mill operates, and its interpretive displays of related equipment and history. Milling grain here began with the aboriginal people, who used hand-operated grinding stones. Although these were improved upon, hand mills were used into the 20th century. Grain was a common crop here, and with constant trade winds sweeping the islands, wind power for grinding the grain was free. The centre follows the evolution of the mill from the traditional stone one through the wooden mills mounted on low buildings. Ask for an English printed guide.

Rte FV20, Tiscamanita. Tel: 928 164 275. Open: Tue–Fri & Sun 9.30am–5.30pm. Admission charge.

Drive: Fuerteventura's historic heart

This circular route leaves the island's golden beaches to explore its historic inland cities and surprisingly steep mountains. Although the route includes narrow mountain roads, these are well surfaced and have guard rails.

Allow three hours' driving time without stops to tour museums.

Begin in Antigua.

1 Antigua

See pp110–11.
Travel north on Rte FV20 for 6km (3³/₄ miles) to La Ampuyenta.

2 La Ampuyenta

The home of a local doctor, is now a museum, representing life in a substantial country house. The chancel of the little church in the village is decorated with murals.

Casa-Museo Dr Mena. Tel: 928 858 998. Open: Tue–Fri & Sun 9.30am–5.30pm. Admission charge.
Continue north 2km (1¹/₄ miles) and turn left onto FV30, signposted to Betancuria. Continue through Llanos de la Concepción to Valle de Santa Inés.

3 Valle de Santa Inés

Watch for signs for craftsmen's workshops along the road, and for the

attractive little **Centro de Artesanía** in Santa Inés. Someone is usually working at an embroidery frame.

Continue south on FV30, climbing to Mirador Morro Velosa, 8km (5 miles).

4 Mirador Morro Velosa

If the mirador gate is closed, continue a few metres further to the lay-by with good views on both sides of the road.

Continue 3km (1³/₄ miles) to Betancuria, noticing the ruined monastery to the left.

5 Betancuria

See pp114–17.

Continue south on FV30, passing on the left the entrance to Parque Rural Aula de la Naturaleza, where there are pine woods, a children's playground and walking trails. About 1km (²/₃ mile) further on is the upper section of Vega del Río Palma.

6 Vega del Río Palma

See p126.

Continue south, climbing to the lay-by at a lookout, 3km (1³/₄ miles).

7 Degollada de los Granadillos

The road reaches a shoulder of **Gran Montaña**, one of the island's highest points at 608m (1,995ft). The views are of the rock-strewn mountainsides, through a cleft to more mountains and the sea far below. A 10-minute walk leads past stone walls to a stand of oddly eroded boulders. Be careful, since the drop on the other side is abrupt. This is not a place for children.

Continue along the corniche road, dropping into Pajara, 7km (4¹/₄ miles).

8 Pájara

See pp122–3.

Continue on FV30 to Tuineje, turning left onto FV20 to Tiscamanita, 16km (10 miles).

9 Tiscamanita

Stop in this little village to visit the excellent **Windmill Interpretive Centre** (*see p123*).

Continue north on FV20 to Valles de Ortega, 10km (6 miles).

10 Valles de Ortega

Part of a group of farming villages – Valles de Ortega and its neighbours are worth a detour. The large church of **San Roque** stands away from the town centre, and if you meander along the side roads just west of the main road, you will see a number of windmills and an aloe-vera farm.

Return to FV20 and continue north to Antigua, 4km (2¹/₂ miles).

Hillside gardens at Santa Inés

Vega del Río Palma

The river Palma referred to in the town's name had more water when the first settlers arrived and planted their farms. It still has enough to maintain the palms along its banks, and the dry river bed is worth following into the lower section of this divided village. Where the road crosses the bridge, the river bed is bordered by rounded and eroded rocks.

The town is a pilgrimage site for the entire island, since it was here that the tiny statue of the Virgen de la Peña was found, under miraculous circumstances. Brought by Béthencourt himself, it had been hidden so well during a pirate attack that it was thought to be lost for nearly a century. On the third Sunday of September, the faithful gather here from all over the island to honour their patron saint.
Rte FV30, 5km (3 miles) south of Betancuria.

Santuario Virgen de la Peña

At the head of the plaza in the upper part of the town stands one of the few churches on the island that does not have a white façade. Faced in local red sandstone, the church is dedicated to Fuerteventura's patron saint. Its high altar is in gold and polychrome with naïve paintings and a fine carved wooden ceiling. Side altars are of carved and painted wood, one with a winged head design that is quite unusual here. Near the side door is another naïve painting, of monks finding the venerated statue. The little alabaster Virgin is now safely housed in the high altar, and it is not unusual to see pilgrims approaching her down the church aisle. The wooden confessional is from the 1400s.
Open: Tue–Sun 11am–1pm & 5–7pm.

Ermita de la Virgen de la Peña

The exact spot of the statue's discovery is now marked by a tiny white chapel. Although it is some distance from the village, and must be approached on foot, the spot is visited all year round by pilgrims. Just beneath the Las Peñitas dam, it is reached by following the road through the lower village and along the edge of the valley until it ends at a path that leads past the silted-up reservoir to the chapel.

Santuario Virgen de la Peña

Ajuy

Atlantic waves pound the cliffs of the headlands at either side of Ajuy, and have worn sea caves at their bases. Between these stretches a black-sand beach where fishing boats are hauled up. Locals and tourists mingle in the two restaurants that overlook the beach; more restaurants are tucked among the houses that climb the steep streets behind it. A walkway leads to the top of the cliffs on the northern end of the beach, to a trail along the headland. In especially rough seas, expect to be showered in sea spray from waves breaking below. The beach at Ajuy was the first landing place of Béthencourt and his party when they arrived to conquer the island.

The road to Ajuy turns north from FV605, 2km (1¼ miles) east of Pájara and 10km (6 miles) south of Vega del Río Palma.

American Star shipwreck

Follow FV605 south from Pájara, taking the right turn towards Playa Solapa – well worth a stop for its sea caves – then follow the shore south to Playa Garcey. Just offshore are the last remains of the ocean liner SS *American Star*. It grounded here in 1994 and attracted many sightseers, but it has now almost completely broken up and been washed away. However, the beach with its riffled sand, the enormous sea arch and the fantastically sculpted puddingstone cliffs are an incredible geological site and worth a visit. Under no circumstances should you try to swim or dive near the wreck: these are dangerous waters.

The interesting beach at Playa Garcey

Southern Fuerteventura

The landscape is one of barren mountains and ragged shore, alternating with long golden strands before ending at the rocky southern tip of the Jandía peninsula. Though bare of greenery, the mountains are striking, as patterns of sunlight and shadow paint them in shades of rose, gold and ochre.

GRAN TARAJAL

Despite tree-lined streets and plazas, Gran Tarajal manages to look more like a pre-tourist port than most, with its narrow streets and passageways climbing from the harbour. Beside the port, a long, black-sand beach is bordered by a new promenade, with cafés, restaurants and tall palm trees. Trees also surround the delightful fountain, with six oversized sea horses spouting water. The adjacent 1879 church was the gift of an emigrant after a successful career in Cuba, who also introduced metal wind pumps to Fuerteventura.

Gran Tarajal is 53km (33 miles) northeast of Morro Jable.

Beaches

Although not really comparable to the magnificent gold-sand beaches of the Jandía peninsula, the coast north of Sotavento de Jandía has its own charms, with beaches tucked into coves between high headlands. Most of these have dark sand, but the headlands offer protection from the wind that sweeps even this leeward side of the island. Along with those in the towns there are a number of small, undeveloped beaches, such as the one along the main road 2km (1 1/4 miles) south of Tarajalejo.

La Lajita

Authentic fishing villages are no longer common on Fuerteventura, so La Lajita is worth a detour. It is a tidy affair, with lots of leafy little parks, and colourful boats line the beach between the two enclosing headlands. A small Lucha Canaria stadium is in the centre of town and a couple of restaurants overlook the beach.

Las Playitas

Another fishing village that retains its character, Las Playitas has some apartments and bungalows, but they do not overwhelm the protected 2.5km (1 1/2-mile) black-sand beach. The little port has a number of good seafood restaurants, too.

Las Playitas is the base for **Cat Company**, which hires out catamarans by the hour and teaches courses at all levels. The sheltered black-sand and pebble beach is especially good for inexperienced sailors.

6.5km (4 miles) northeast of Gran Tarajal. Las Playitas Grand Resort. Tel: 616 619 313. www.catcompany.eu. Open: daily 10am–6pm.

Oasis Park

The main road passes through the botanical gardens at Oasis Park, which has an entrance from the bus stop and another further south for cars. It really is an oasis, with pathways through a forest of tropical trees and shrubs, and lush borders of scented geranium. Over 2,000 varieties of cactus are shown in a separate hillside garden, and camel rides are offered at the edge of the oasis. The wildlife park features raptor and parrot shows, as well as a collection of reptiles, primates, elephants, giraffes, hippos and sealife. If you plan on seeing the parrot show, be sure to ask at the entrance.

Rte FV2, La Lajita. Tel: 928 161 135. Open: daily 9am–6pm. Admission charge to gardens; free entrance to the huge plant nursery.

Camel rides on offer at Oasis Park

Tarajalejo

Fishing village turned low-key holiday centre, Tarajalejo is appealing for its relaxed air and water sports. Constant winds and moderate water temperatures make this coast ideal for sailing.

Tarajalejo is 40km (25 miles) northeast of Morro Jable.

SOTAVENTO AND COSTA CALMA

Expect to be thoroughly confused by all the names by which this coast – and each town along it – are known. Road signs, map names and common usage differ widely and are in constant flux. The name Costa Calma can mean either the made-for-tourists complex or an entire string of beaches (also known as Jandía and Sotavento). Developers assign names to new urbanisations with no regard to the town that might have been there before, leaving mapmakers as confused as travellers.

Whatever their names, these beaches – some 30km (19 miles) of them – together with those in the Corralejo Dunes are some of the finest in the Canary Islands; *the* finest, according to many. Never mind that some are backed by impossible encrustations of hotels and apartments that leave not a spot of land showing; there are still plenty with beautiful sand backed by cliffs or dunes.

Beaches

By far the most beautiful section of beach is Playa de Sotavento, stretching for several kilometres south of Costa Calma. Wide and white, it has a lagoon enclosed by a sandbar, and an almost endless expanse of sand. More beaches spread to the south, with the final long strand at the northern end of Morro Jable.

Sotavento means 'leeward', and this is the more protected coast of the Jandía peninsula. That said, don't expect the air to be still. These beaches are subject to the almost constant winds that sweep the entire island, but the surf is more gentle and the wind not quite so strong on this side.

To reach Playa de Sotavento, take the turning off FV2 south of Costa Calma signposted to Hotel Los Gorriones and continue to the end.

Mountains protect the coast

Costa Calma

Opinions are sharply divided on this new tourist hotel 'town', the most common being, to quote Gertrude Stein, that 'there's no there there'. Lacking in local character and with few good restaurants or entertainment venues outside the hotels, this resort is the domain of the all-inclusive packages. The quality of hotels varies widely and most agree that the resort is for those whose main interest is beach or pool, and who do not require nightlife or a choice of restaurants. However, Costa Calma has incredible beaches, and it hosts the international windsurfing and kitesurfing championships in July.

Jandía Mountain

Rising behind the idyllic beaches is the long ridge of Monte Jandía, rising to the island's highest elevation at 807m (2,648ft). Various tracks meander up its desert-like slopes, most accessible only to four-wheel-drive vehicles.

Mirador del Sotavento

To get a sense of the size of Playa de Sotavento de Jandía, view it from the south, from a mirador just past Casas Risco Paso. The view up the coast includes the desert mountainside dropping to the beach below, bordered in water of an ultramarine shade so deep that it looks painted. From here there's a bird's-eye view of the wide beach and the lagoon that divides it.

Lush vegetation overlooking the beach at Costa Calma

Windsurfing

By far the most popular water sport in the Canaries is windsurfing. The average reliability rate for winds is around 50 per cent in winter and 60–75 per cent in summer. Lanzarote is windier than Fuerteventura, but for wave-sailing conditions, Fuerteventura is the better choice.

On Fuerteventura, the beaches of Playa de Sotavento de Jandía draw devotees of the sport from all over the world. The annual world championship speed finals are held at Playa de Sotavento in July and August, and, with wind speeds up to force 9, contestants fly across the waves. International Speed Weeks are also held here. The centre of activity is the Procenter F2 school at Hotel Los Gorriones.

But Sotavento is not the only beach to try. The whole length of the Costa

There is plenty of windsurfing instruction available in the Canaries

Calma from Bahía Calma south to Morro Jable is one long, beautiful beach. Look for Playa Esmeralda, Casas Risco del Paso, Butihondo and Playa del Matorral, all of which offer good conditions. Further north along the coast try Playa del Castillo at Caleta de Fuste, Playa de Lajas at Puerto Lajas and Flag Beach and Playa Bajo Negro on the dunes south of Corralejo.

The western side of Fuerteventura has the strongest winds but is noted for its treacherous currents. Only the strongest should attempt windsurfing here, but conditions can also be thrilling. El Cotillo is popular with experienced windsurfers, but this beach has a reputation for breaking gear! Do not windsurf alone here, as there are no rescue services.

Lanzarote has fewer noted places but some good conditions. The Lanzarote Surf Company, at Costa Teguise, is another F2 centre where the surfing reaches epic speeds. One of the most popular, but difficult, spots is at La Caleta de Famara, a huge bay nestled under towering mountains – but it's not for the faint-hearted! There are two windsurfing shops at Famara which have rental gear and instruction. While some find the waters off Jameos del Agua challenging, only the most experienced should sail there. There are no sandy beaches and the coarse lava rock can chew you up quickly, so be sure to wear appropriate footwear. Beginners may want to get lessons at Club La Santa, north of La Santa on the north coast.

Windsurfing is a popular pastime at Parque Natural de Corralejo

If you are a beginner or even an intermediate, be sure to seek out instruction and advice on the best places for a person of your skill level. Windsurfing centres can be found near all of the major surf spots and even along the promenade at Arrecife.

MORRO JABLE

The only real town on this coast, Morro Jable has a seriously split personality. The main town lies on either side of a deep *barranco* (ravine) that divides it in two. Beyond, a steep headland hides the old town from the fishing port. More recently, a tourist development has been growing along the beach to its north, and, to confuse things even further, this new section is more commonly known in tourist publications as Jandía.

Morro Jable's previous life as a fishing village gives it an old-world charm, its narrow streets lined with white buildings dropping steeply to the shore. There's a pleasant promenade by the water, with a choice of cafés and good seafood restaurants.

65km (40 miles) southwest of the airport.

Beach

The 4km- (2^1/$_2$ mile-) long beach, Playa del Matorral (also known as Playa de Jandía), which not long ago had only a few beach bars, has been transformed into a tourist colony. Its wide promenade is lined with shops, cafés and restaurants, mostly catering for German tastes. Creeping ever higher up the mountain behind it is a dense concentration of hotels, seemingly stacked upon each other's roofs. It's a hotchpotch of styles and architecture, built without regard to streets, that would leave a city planner speechless. This part of town holds a Thursday market (*9am–1pm*), but it sells virtually nothing with any Canarian connection. (*Tourist information, Avda. de Saladar. Tel: 928 540 776. Open: Mon–Fri 8am–3pm.*)

A boardwalk leads from the main road across the tidal pools to the beach, passing directly beneath the lighthouse, **Faro del Matorral**. A restaurant overlooks the beach from a little rise; sunbeds and parasols may be hired here.

On the beach and along the esplanade are centres and equipment for sailing, windsurfing, parasailing and diving, making this a well-rounded beach for water activities. Along the promenade is **Subcat**, where you can book places on a completely submergible catamaran that does one-

Faro del Matorral

hour trips reaching a depth of 30m/100ft but you won't see much sealife (*Avda. de Saladar 1. Tel: 928 166 392. www.subcat-fuerteventura.com. Open: 9am–1.30pm & 3.30–7pm*).

Hire a bicycle at **Servicios Unifuer**, a few doors north, to cycle to the far end of the beach (*Centro Comercial Ventura Jandía. Tel: 928 541 584*).

Fishing harbour

You can often see fishermen unloading their catch at the harbour, or you can join a day trip yourself:

Magic is a day-cruise catamaran offering whale and dolphin sightings, stops for swimming, a free bar and jet-skiing (*Tel: 900 506 260, 928 150 248*).

Blue Nose runs deep-sea fishing trips (*Tel: 628 021 451*).

Bala Roja runs excursions to inaccessible coves and beaches in a large Zodiac boat (*Tel: 928 541 771*).

Pedra Santaña thrills youngsters with a pirate-themed cruise, while adults appreciate the chance to sail on the 1940 sailing vessel. This was one of the last sailing vessels used commercially in Spain, working the north coast until the 1960s. On board passengers will learn to tie seamen's knots, play games and have a chance to go snorkelling. The trip also includes lunch (*Puerto del Morro Jable. Tel (mobile): 670 745 191. Sails: Mon–Sat*).

The *Pedra Santaña* moored in Morro Jable harbour

Drive: Jandía peninsula

The southern tip of the Jandía peninsula is seldom visited by package tourists. Its sandy stretches are difficult to reach and often dangerous, and much of the road is unsealed, but the trip outlined here is easily accessible by car. It offers a rare view of the other side of this lonely point. Take water and also a picnic, or plan to stop at one of the three restaurants en route.

Allow two hours' driving time.

Start at Puerto del Morro Jable.

1 Puerto del Morro Jable
See pp134–5.
Leave the port, turning sharp left near the top of the hill. There are excellent views down to the harbour from here, before the road begins its twisting climb to a plateau. Continue to the sign for *Punta del Viento, 9km (5¹/₂ miles).*

2 Punta del Viento
The winding road finally levels out above the rocky shore, punctuated by a series of points, each marked by a sign.

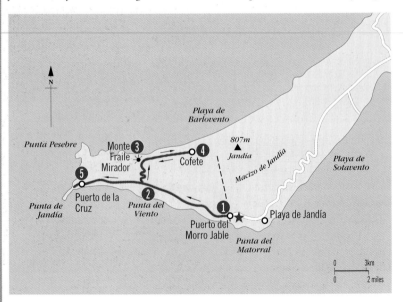

Goats wander among the rocks in search of greenery, and an occasional abandoned farm breaks the landscape. *Continue to the right turning, signposted to Cofete, 3km (1³/₄ miles).*

3 Monte Fraile Mirador

Leaving the coast, the roads begins to climb again, over a shoulder of Monte Fraile, part of the Jandía ridge. At the crest is a lookout. Here is the first sight of the wild, deserted Playa de Barlovento, an unbroken line of gold sand and rolling breakers beloved by surfers. Above it rises the steep northern side of Jandía mountain, really a whole ridge of jagged peaks, eroded, rock-strewn and entirely forbidding. Only an occasional tentative brush of green relieves the barren slopes.

Backtrack from here, or continue down the other side to Cofete, 9km (5¹/₂ miles).

4 Cofete

One restaurant and a cluster of houses is about all there is to this outpost, apart from the abandoned **Villa Winter**, which was built before World War II by a German, Gustav Winter, who was supposedly given this land by General Franco for services rendered. He was also a Nazi sympathiser and it is rumoured, among other things, that this was a halfway house for war criminals fleeing to South America. Although the tracks that head towards the shore are not safe for any but four-wheel-drive vehicles, they are good for walking, as is the long golden beach. It is not safe to swim here, however, because of the unchecked Atlantic currents and heavy surf, which has claimed the lives of a number of swimmers.

Return over the mountain to the junction near Punta del Viento, turning right and continuing 9km (5¹/₂ miles).

5 Puerto de la Cruz

The road ends at the lonely lighthouse on Punta de Jandía. Deserted and barred, the lighthouse has been the subject of several plans for rehabilitation. The village of Puerto de la Cruz consists of a clutch of white and yellow buildings atop a low cliff, and two restaurants here serve good fish dishes.

Return to Puerto del Morro Jable, 11km (7 miles).

Puerto del Morro Jable

Drive: Jandía peninsula

Getting away from it all

Getting away from the crowds is never a problem on either Lanzarote or Fuerteventura, once you leave the resort centres. The very fact that most tourist facilities are grouped into these mega-complexes (which are really quite small in comparison to other more famous sunspots) means that the overwhelming majority of tourists gather there. That leaves the rest pretty much to the curious traveller, who can hire a car and explore.

ADVENTURE EXCURSIONS
Air explorations

Viewing Timanfaya's line of volcanoes from the air is an unforgettable experience. Not only does it give a different perspective on the landscape, but it complements the land tour offered by the park.

Lanza Air One-hour tours of the island, especially the volcanoes.
Avda. Islas Canarias, Los Charcos Local 8, Costa Teguise. Tel: 928 806 215. Open: 9am–2pm.

Heli-Tour Service Helicopters seating six passengers make 30- and 50-minute trips.
Tel: 676 701 693.

Boat trips

A wide variety of boat excursions is offered at most of the larger coastal tourist resorts, providing a different view of the islands, and often also a chance to participate in activities without the bother of driving. These include a variety of water craft, with sailing yachts, motor launches, catamarans, glass-hulled boats and sailing sloops. There are even submarines that conduct hour-long cruises to see underwater life, but these are more for novelty than for what you will actually see of the ocean's wildlife. Many providers will arrange for your transfer from your hotel to the boat. If you would prefer to skipper your own course, it's easy to charter a boat from pleasure marinas or yacht clubs.

Lanzarote

Ana Segundo Hourly water bus service between Puerto Calero and Puerto del Carmen.
Puerto del Carmen harbour & Puerto Calero. Tel: 928 514 322, 629 731 293. Sails: 10.30am, 12.30pm, 3pm & 5pm.

Catlanza The catamaran operates full-day cruises to the Papagayo beaches, and includes refreshment on the way, swimming, snorkelling, beach activities including free jet-ski instruction and full lunch.

Puerto Calero. *Tel: 928 513 022.*
www.catlanza.com
Cesar II
Full-day cruises from Lanzarote to
the dunes and beaches south of
Corralejo on Fuerteventura, plus
Isla de Lobos for swimming,
snorkelling, banana boat rides and
other water activities.
*Solymar Cruceros, Calle José Antonio 90,
Arrecife. Tel: 928 813 608. Sails: Mon–
Fri, departs 10.15am, returns 5.45pm.*
Marea Errota Day sails on a two-
masted schooner, with stops for
swimming and snorkelling at the
Papagayo beaches.
*Playa Blanca, Playa Blanca harbour.
Tel: 928 517 633, 676 965 403.
http://personal2.iddeo.es/mareaerrota.
Sails: Tue–Fri 10.45am–3.45pm.*
Ocean Cat A number of options
include adventures in the waters of
both Lanzarote and Fuerteventura,
from mini-cruises out of Puerto del
Carmen to day-long cruises that
include the beaches of Fuerteventura
and Isla de Lobos. They pick up
at hotels.

Getting away from it all

Submarine excursions from Puerto Calero

*Calle El Teide 30, Puerto del Carmen.
Tel: 928 512 323. www.oceancatt.com*
Princesa Ico The glass-bottomed
catamaran cruises to the Corralejo
dunes and beaches, with hotel
pick-up.
*Puerto del Carmen. Tel: 928 514 322, 629
731 293. www.princesaico.com. Sails:
multiple sailings daily, from 8.45am.*
Sea Breeze Charters Full-day and
longer charter cruises on the 10m (33ft)
ketch *Sea Breeze*, with a full-time crew.
Puerto Calero. Tel: 619 734 215.
Submarine Safaris One-hour
explorations under the sea in a 48-
passenger boat are more for novelty
than for undersea life.
*Puerto Calero. Tel: 928 512 898.
www.submarinesafaris.com*

Fuerteventura
Celia Cruz A glass-bottomed
catamaran offering a large variety of
excursions, including trips to Isla de
Lobos and Papagayo beaches.
Puerto de Corralejo. Tel: 639 140 014.
Excursiones Maritimas The least
expensive way to get to Isla de Lobos,
on a 45-minute cruise.
*Puerto de Corralejo. Sails: 10.15am,
11.45am & 3.30pm, returns: 10.30am,
noon & 4pm.*
Oceancat The catamaran sails to the
island of Los Lobos on a full-day trip
that includes a barbecue, snorkelling,
swimming, open bar and jet-ski.
Puerto de Corralejo. Tel: 627 537 580.
Oceano A 16m (52ft) ketch, which you
can charter or join as a day-cruise

The Puerto del Carmen beaches

Cycling Timanfaya's trails is a rewarding experience

passenger. Whale and dolphin sightings are fairly common, and the boat stops for swimming.

Port of Morro Jable. Tel: 649 984 406. Sails: daily, with free hotel transfer.

Subcat A completely submergible catamaran that does one-hour trips reaching a depth of 30m (98ft).

Avda. de Saladar 1, Jandía. Tel: 928 166 392.

Bicycles

These are available for hire from most major resorts. Only the very fit will attempt the mountainous inland routes, but Lanzarote and Fuerteventura both offer a reasonable amount of flat terrain to explore. Bikers should bear in mind that the roads on the island are very narrow and there are no bicycle lanes nor paved verges. The good news is that traffic is light. Fuerteventura is the more mountainous of the two islands, and the plains around Antigua are the easiest for cycling. There are some fine, less stressful, sections on Lanzarote, but hills are apt to be long. There is a nice area for cycling surrounding the La Santa, Sóo and La Caleta de Famara area. Bike hire is available in most resorts.

Lanzarote

Bike Station *Centro Comercial Maretas (near the post office), Costa Teguise. Tel: 628 102 177. www.mylanzarote.com*

Famara Surf *Avda. Marinero 39, La Caleta de Famara. Tel: 928 528 676. www.famarasurf.com*

Renner Bikes *Centro Comercial Marítimo (upper floor), Avda. de las Playas, Puerto del Carmen.* *Tel: 928 510 612, mobile: 629 990 755.* *www.mountainbike-lanzarote.com*

Fuerteventura
Vulcano Biking *Calle Acorazado España 8, Corralejo. Tel: 928 535 706.*

Horse riding

Trail rides head inland or along the shore to beaches inaccessible by car, a good way to explore off the beaten track. The following establishments offer instruction as well as rides:

Lanzarote
Lanzarote a Caballo *Rte LZ2, near Uga.* *Tel: 928 830 038.*
Rancho Texas Equestrian Centre *Puerto del Carmen (signs from Playa de los Pocillos). Tel: 928 841 286.*

Kayak tours

Lanza-Canoa *Tel: 928 522 989, mobile: 616 771 440. www.lanza-canoa.com* Tours include the bridges of Arrecife, the coast and beaches of Puerto del Carmen, the rocks and beaches of Playa Blanca's Papagayo, and the caves and coves of Playa Quemada. Guided tours are by multilingual staff. Independent kayakers can rent kayaks, which Lanza-Canoa will deliver.

BEACHES

Fuerteventura and Lanzarote have rocky, lava-ridden coastlines, but scattered along the shore between rocky points and headlands are beaches small and large, with yellow sand, black sand or cobble. And in some places these beaches stretch literally for kilometres. Fuerteventura is a beach lover's paradise, with endless golden sands allowing space for everyone – sunbathers, windsurfers, surfers, and, on the protected beaches, swimmers and the bucket-and-spade set.

Confronted by all this golden sand and deep blue water, it is important to remember where you are – in the open Atlantic Ocean, where currents are both strong and dangerous. If you are on a solitary beach, particularly one facing north or west (this applies to all the islands), enter the water with great caution, if at all. Currents can be treacherous, and a number of holidaymakers seeking solitude on the west coast of Fuerteventura have come to grief. If you swim in the ocean, swim parallel to the shore, and always ask locally about the safety of the waters.

Some of the best beaches are among the dunes just south of Corralejo on Fuerteventura and in the long sandy stretches of the Costa Calma dunes above Morro Jable.

On the southern end of Lanzarote, in the Monumento Natural de los Ajaches, are the Papagayo beaches, possibly the most beautiful on the island, although these can get crowded. The beaches on La Graciosa, off the north end of Lanzarote, and Isla de Lobos, opposite Corralejo on Fuerteventura, are good for escaping the crowds. You will also find attractive beaches at Puerto del Carmen, at Playa Honda near the airport and at Costa Teguise where there are a number of smaller beaches.

ISLETS

Although most guides will tell you that there are seven Canary Islands, there are really thirteen. Among the islets that don't feature in the tourist brochures are Isla de Lobos, opposite Corralejo on Fuerteventura, and La Graciosa, Montaña Clara and Alegranza, all to the north of Lanzarote.

Regular ferries run to Lobos and La Graciosa. You can walk round Lobos in just over two hours, and, apart from a few other curious tourists, you won't see a soul, as no one lives here. The main attraction is the beach and a pretty lagoon – and perfect picnic and

swimming spots. By comparison, La Graciosa (*see pp86–7*) is busier. There are two tiny settlements here, and you can even stay overnight in a pension. The beaches are superb, but the currents make them dangerous for swimming.

To get to the other, tiny, island rocks (further north), you will need an accommodating fishing boat. Ask on La Graciosa, or at Orzola on Lanzarote. Alegranza is approximately half the size of La Graciosa, at 10sq km (4sq miles), and lies 20km (12$^{1}/_{2}$ miles) off the north coast of Lanzarote. There is a tiny fishing community here, but, unless you're a birdwatcher, little else to warrant the trip. Montaña Clara (just off La Graciosa) is the smallest of all at just 1sq km ($^{1}/_{3}$ sq mile). It's also the most spectacular, with a 256m- (840ft-) high volcano at its heart.

Space to stretch out at Playa del Matorral, Jandía

JEEP SAFARIS

It is hard to look at this scenery without wanting to get off the road and explore it more closely. One way to do this is by taking a jeep safari. These outfitters explore tracks that most drivers would hesitate to follow (especially in a hired car, where insurance may exclude unpaved roads). The downside, however, is that the back of a jeep is hard and cramped – and particularly uncomfortable in inclement weather. Make sure that the operator is able to provide commentary on the sights you are passing and don't hesitate to ask him/her to slow down if the going is rough. Jeep excursions are available through a number of operators, and are widely advertised. If you go, take precautions to avoid sunburn and dehydration.

If you rent your own 4×4 car or quad, you must keep on the dirt paths as, although it seems barren desert, most birds nestle among the rocks and bushes.

WALKING

If you really want to leave the crowds behind, one way is to walk. Although these islands may not seem ideal for the casual walker, with daunting, rough-surfaced terrain and few waymarked trails, some of the trail walks are quite exceptional. One of Lanzarote's best-kept secrets is the free walking tour provided by ICONA, the Spanish nature conservancy organisation, in the Parque Nacional de Timanfaya. You must telephone ahead to book your place, but on this walk you can enjoy an insider's view of some of the finest scenery on Lanzarote (*see pp54–5*). Walkers are met by trained naturalists at the Visitors' Centre and taken by van to the trailhead. Book early, as only seven participants can go on each of the thrice-weekly walks.

Although you are not allowed to leave the car in most of the park, there are a few places where you can walk unguided. To learn about these, ask at the Visitor's Centre for the trail leaflet, which describes three walks, both inside and adjacent to the park. One explores the park's rocky shoreline, and the other climbs go to the rim of a volcano. Be sure to have them mark the way to the trailheads on a map; without this, you would never find them.

A splendid place for a self-guided walk is at the Monumento Natural de los Ajaches on the south end of the island near Playa Blanca. It is a huge area with a multitude of trails over and around the stark cliffs that surround the park's outstanding beaches. You'll need stout walking shoes (boots are best) for walks of any length, plus water, a sunhat, and a wind jacket if you are walking at high altitudes. Never walk alone, and always tell someone where you are going and when you expect to be back.

On Fuerteventura, a part of the ancient path leading to Corralejo has been restored, taking you from Lajares alongside the volcano Hondo, where it connects to a path up to the rim of the crater (*see pp106–7*). This is part of a long-term project to promote nature tourism by creating a walking trail that runs the entire length of the island. This is in the process of being built and signposted.

Walking tours

Surprisingly, there are very few commercial walking tour operators.

Lanzarote
Canary Trekking *Calle La Laguna 18, Casa 1, Costa Teguise.*
Tel: 696 900 929, 609 537 684.
www.canarytrekking.com

Fuerteventura
Caminata Walks that focus particularly on the flora and fauna of the island.
Villa Boicana, Villaverde.
Tel: 928 535 010.

The north of Lanzarote is ideal walking country

Shopping

Few would suggest a shopping holiday on either island, but that's not to say that shopping can't be an enjoyable part of your trip. The first lesson to learn when shopping in the Canaries is to ignore all those 'tax-free' and 'duty-free' signs. The islands were declared a duty-free zone in 1852 by the Spanish authorities in order to stimulate trade, and that ever since then they have retained certain privileges; you will enjoy one of these when you buy petrol, which is cheap.

The islands are now in fact designated a 'trade-free' zone, which means they are free of certain import taxes, but these benefits are not necessarily passed on to the customer.

The luxury goods on which favourable tax rates apply are typically cameras, jewellery, perfume, leather items, tobacco and spirits. The last two are certainly bargains, but elsewhere there is often little to choose between Canarian shops, international airport duty-free shop prices and those at home. The best rule is to know the best price of these goods at home before you leave – prices in duty-free shops are often no different – or even higher.

Island products

The best souvenirs from a trip are those traditionally made on the islands, sometimes right before your eyes: baskets, straw hats, wood carvings, pottery, rugs and embroidered tableware. You will find *centros artesanías* (craft workshops) throughout the islands but, like quality crafts at home, you should not expect these handmade items to be cheap. This is because many hours' labour goes into them (unlike the machine-produced Far East imports you will see sold at the street markets and in some shops).

Are those table linens in the markets made in the Canary Islands? Probably not, unless you buy them at the Saturday market in Haría, where all the exhibitors are island craftspeople or farm producers. Those in *artesanías* are also made by local craftspeople. The rest are most probably not.

Another local product that you may find useful while you are still on the islands is the variety of aloe-vera skin creams. This healing plant is grown on farms (one is near Rte FV50, southeast of Antigua) and harvested to make skin lotions, complexion creams and medical products, especially those to treat burns. If spending too long on the beach leaves you with sunburn, head for the aloe cream.

Don't overlook food and drink as interesting presents or tasty souvenirs. On both Fuerteventura and Lanzarote these include *mojo* sauces (*see pp162–3*), cactus jellies or honey in small gift packs, and wines you can sample in the *bodegas* of Lanzarote. Fuerteventura's aged goats' cheeses are another treat to consider, as is the excellent smoked salmon from Yaiza, which comes packed to travel.

Markets

The most colourful shopping in the Canaries takes place on Lanzarote, when everyone descends on the Sunday market at Teguise. You'll find just about everything there except locally made handicrafts, which are in short supply among the cheap imports. The event at Teguise, which is something of a weekly carnival, is as important as the merchandise, featuring folk dancing, Canarian wrestling demonstrations and street performers.

Smaller markets, also selling heavily or exclusively imported goods, are in Corralejo, Caleta de Fuste and Jandía on Fuerteventura, and at Costa Teguise (Friday) on Lanzarote. For quality handicrafts try the market in Tetir, Fuerteventura, every other Sunday morning, or see the Haría market (*see p149*).

Colourful shopping at the market at Teguise

Pottery from the Centro Artesanía de Haría

Shops

Normal shop opening hours are Monday to Saturday 9am or 10am to 1pm or 2pm, and 4pm or 5pm to 7pm or 8pm. In resorts, nearly all shops and supermarkets stay open all day until 10pm.

Where to buy

Lanzarote

Teguise, home to the popular Sunday market and a good choice of quality shops, is possibly the most popular, but certainly not the only, place to buy. Elsewhere, the island maintains a tasteful arty image, with designer goods, the work of local artists and its famous wines, which you can sample and buy from *bodegas* in La Geria.

Ahumaderia Uga A highly regarded salmon smoker, where you can sample and buy smoked salmon, packaged to travel.

Rte LZ2, Uga. Tel: 928 830 132. Open: Tue–Fri 10am–1.30pm & 4–6.30pm, Sat 10am–2pm.

Casa Kaos Artisans are individually showcased, including those who work in sand casting, peridot and black volcanic rock jewellery, ironwork, traditional and modern pottery, art glass and a wide variety of others. One of the best sources of quality original local crafts on the island.

Calle León y Castillo 2, Teguise. Tel: 928 845 597.

Eckhoff Collection Tiny shop shows handiwork of local and expat artists in Haría, including wines and condiments using locally grown products.

Longuera 22 (opposite the artisans' co-op), Haría. Tel: 928 835 761.

Fundación César Manrique Manrique designs on beach towels, silk scarves and ceramics, along with framed graphics.

Taro de Tahiche, 5km (3 miles) north of Arrecife. Tel: 928 843 138/928 843 070. www.fcmanrique.org. Open: Mon–Sat 10am–6pm, Sun 10am–3pm (winter); daily 10am–7pm (summer).

Galería La Villa A series of small shops featuring designer fashions, quality Moroccan goods and silk clothing.

Plaza Clavijo y Fajardo 4, Teguise.
Open: Tue–Fri 11am–2pm & 5–7.30pm,
Sun 10am–2pm.

Galería Yaiza Small gallery selling
original paintings, sculpture, weaving
and pottery.
Rte LZ2, Yaiza. Tel: 928 830 199.
Open: Mon–Sat evenings.

Handicrafts Centre Traditional crafts
are demonstrated and sold in studios,
including pottery, baskets, weaving and
pulled-thread work.
Monumento al Campesino, Mozaga, 8km
(5 miles) northwest of Arrecife.
Tel: 928 520 136. Open: daily 10am–5pm;
restaurant open noon–4.30pm; tapas bar
open 10am–5.45pm.

Haría Artisans Market The best weekly
crafts market on the islands, entirely
composed of local craftspeople or food
producers selling high-quality
traditional needlecrafts, handmade
costume dolls, sand painting, jewellery
and locally made foods.
Plaza León y Castillo, Haría. Open: Sat
10am–2pm.

Museo del Visitante A very good,
although small, museum gift shop
with tasteful gift items not available
elsewhere.
LZ67, Mancha Blanca, 3km (1¾ miles)
south of Tinajo. Tel: 928 840 831. Open:
daily 9am–5pm.

Taller de Artesanía Chiche Creative
and aboriginal ceramic works and
glass-bead making. An in-house artist
can be seen at work.
In the centre of town in Mager, Haría.
Tel: (676) 811 429.

Fuerteventura

Centro de Artesanía Demonstrations
and sale of traditional Canarian
embroidery and other crafts, at very
reasonable prices.
Rte FV30, Santa Inés.

Centro de Artesanía Traditional crafts
displayed, sold and demonstrated
include pottery, weaving, basketry,
pulled-thread work and sometimes the
playing of traditional musical
instruments.
Plaza Santa María, Betancuria.
Open: Mon–Sat 11am–4pm.

Straw hats for sale at Haría market

Ecomuseo de La Alcogida One of the farmhouses at this village has been converted to craft workshops, in many of which are demonstrations (and sales) of Canarian pulled-thread embroidery, tin working, basketry, weaving, leatherwork, pottery and stone cutting. *Rte FV207, just south of Tefía.* *Tel: 928 175 343. Open: Tue–Fri & Sun 9.30am–5.30pm.*

Escuela de Artesanía Canaria

Sra Hernández Demonstrations of intricate pulled-thread embroidery at an active school where the art is taught and practised regularly. An excellent selection of handmade needlework is for sale, from handkerchiefs and serviettes to entire sets of table linen, all locally made. *Plaza Santa María, Lajares.* *Open: Mon–Fri 9am–7pm,* *Sat 9am–3pm. Free admission.*

Feria Insular de Artesanía The island's major folk-life festival features traditional craftspeople demonstrating and selling. *Antigua, early May.*

Molino de Antigua An excellent craft shop displaying and selling traditional and contemporary crafts, one of the finest selections anywhere in the Canary Islands. Fine examples of pulled-thread embroidery, woven palm baskets and hats, terracotta pottery based on designs of the prehistoric inhabitants, excellent woodcarving, handweaving, tinwork, painted silk

ISLAND CRAFTS

The most common traditional crafts are those closest to the daily needs of rural families: spinning and weaving for clothing and household goods, basket work for hats and containers, stone working for buildings, and metalwork in both iron and tin for containers, tools, farm equipment and building hardware. Ironically, perhaps the one craft that is best known as associated with the islands is a purely ornamental and decorative one – the delicate and lovely openwork embroidery.

Spinning and weaving came to the island with the arrival of sheep, brought by the conquistadors. Today's craftsmen still work in natural sheep wool, often combined with a cotton warp in heavier items such as rag rugs. Some of the most popular small items are square, flat shoulder bags in natural wool, often in black-and-white plaids.

Fuerteventura is known for its woven palm-leaf baskets and hats, once basic requirements for any family. Today these are mostly for display, although the baskets are practical containers. Some hats are designed to shade the face – such as those you'll see worn by women working on farms – but more often they are the small costume hats tied over headscarves and seen only on folk dancers.

The same practical items that tinsmiths have traditionally made everywhere – lamps, watering cans, lanterns, candlesticks, buckets and funnels – are still made by island craftsmen, although now mostly for decorative purposes.

Of all the crafts, wrought-ironwork has moved with the greatest ease into the world of modern art. Like spinning and weaving, this art and its materials arrived with the conquerors, and was used to forge farm equipment, tools, knives, horseshoes, keys, locks, latches and hinges. As these items became available readymade, ironworkers turned their talents to designing decorative but useful furniture, lamps and other items.

scarves, silver jewellery, in all styles from the oldest island traditions to stunning modern designs.

Rte FV20, north of Antigua.
Tel: 928 878 041. Open: Tue–Fri & Sun 9.30am–5.30pm.

A traditional sand painting

Entertainment

Even in resort areas where there is a good quantity of entertainment, quality and variety are invariably disappointing, with an overabundance of grotesque home-from-home 'fun pubs'. Don't expect the spectaculars with showgirls and gala stage sets. High-end hotels such as Melia Salinas in Costa Teguise or the Blue Bay Palace in Corralejo may have good shows, but 'evening entertainment' advertised in the promotionals for most resorts is more likely to be a rousing game of bingo.

MUSIC AND NIGHTLIFE

Clubs and live music bars seem, oddly, to be in best supply in Corralejo, on Fuerteventura. A few of the larger resort towns have some: ask at your hotel for the current possibilities.

The easiest way to shop for live shows is to wander in the resort towns; most places are open to the street, so you can stand outside for a while to sample the music or comedian before you enter.

Lanzarote
Costa Teguise

Avenida de las Islas Canarias has the highest concentration of venues, and the Plaza at Pueblo Marinero often has performers, usually British bands. The Lighthouse, on Calle Olas, has live acts on the terrace.

Puerto del Carmen

Most places are along Avenida de las Playas, including Joker and Cesar's (where there are nightclub-style dancing-girl shows). The shopping centre, Biosfere Plaza on Avenida Juan Carlos, has several bars with music (and air conditioning). Nearer the old harbour, La Bodega, on Calle Roque Nuble, has a Spanish guitar trio. Up the hill, on Calle Reina Sofía, the Purple Turtle draws a crowd for its Brit comedy acts.

Fuerteventura

In the north of the island, La Oliva and Corralejo, there are three important annual events to which tourists are welcome: the Blues Festival in March, the Dunas Short Film Festival in May and the Fuerteventura Jazz Festival in September.

Caleta de Fuste

Although a little quieter and classier, Caleta has some entertainment along Calle Soto Morales, including Portuguese Fado and Spanish flamenco shows. Legends, in Los Arcos, offers live 60s music most nights.

Corralejo

With a hotter nightlife scene than any other town, Corralejo's scene is aimed primarily at the young surfer set. Rock Island Bar (*www.rockislandbar.com*) has live acoustic music, and Sadie's, on Calle Isaac Peral in the old town, has live drag shows most nights, while Golden Days offers live entertainment every night. Several places cluster in the Centro Comercial Atlántico, where there are bars aplenty, including Bubbles, a gay bar, and Coyote, both discos on the top floor offering everything from R&B to hip-hop. Irish/British pubs are to be found on every street – there are more than 30 British bars in Corralejo!

FLAMENCO

Though it has nothing to do with the Canaries, flamenco shows are occasionally staged by the top hotels, and more rarely in bars and restaurants. The Montaña Tropical Centre, Calle Toscón, Puerto del Carmen, Lanzarote, hosts regular flamenco.

FOLKLORE

Canarian folklore shows are low-key but enjoyable family affairs, with large groups of musicians accompanying a dance troupe in traditional costume. The rhythms are generally Spanish, played on guitars, flutes, and the timple, a small ukulele-like instrument. The best shows are staged in the famous Lanzarote attraction, Jameos del Agua, where there are folklore evenings every Tuesday, Friday and Saturday night (*Tel: 928 848 020*).

Folkloric shows are sometimes held at Monumento al Campesino, in Mozaga, 8km (5 miles) northwest of Arrecife (*Tel: 928 520 136*).

Traditional country dancing at Teguise market

Children

Either island can provide an ideal family holiday. Canarians, like the mainland Spanish, love children, and you will rarely have any trouble taking even small children into restaurants or café-bars. Many hotels have special pools for children, and larger resort hotels have daily programmes and play centres with qualified staff and planned activities, so parents can have a little well-earned time to themselves.

Go-karting

Children as young as five can enjoy go-karting with adults at the **Gran Karting Club**; older kids have their own karts and tracks.
Rte LZ7, km 7, Arrecife, Lanzarote. www.grankarting.com

Playgrounds

All towns have well-equipped public playgrounds; La Oliva has an especially good one near the church.

'Safaris' and nature parks

Children can take animal rides on a camel, donkey or horse, or visit exotic birds or caves.

Lanzarote

Cueva de los Verdes A chance to explore a volcanic cave.
26km (16 miles) north of Arrecife. Tel: 928 848 484. Open: daily 10am–6pm (last tour 6pm).
Echadero de los Camellos (Camel Park) 15-minute camel rides on a volcanic

cone. *Parque de Timanfaya, 3km (1³/₄ miles) north of Yaiza. Open: daily 9am–5.45pm.*
Guinate Tropical Park A 'jungle' experience with exotic birds and animals.
Guinate, 1km (²/₃ mile) from Rte LZ10, 5km (3 miles) north of Haría. Tel: 928 835 500. Open: daily 10am–5pm.
Lanzarote a Caballo Camel, prairie wagon and pony rides.
Rte LZ2. Tel: 928 830 038. www.lanzaroteacaballo.com. Open: daily.

Fuerteventura

Acuario del Mar Colourful fish and other marine creatures.
Rte FV-1 Tarajalejo. Tel: 928 872 070. Open: daily 10am–7pm.
La Lajita Oasis Park Botanic gardens and exotic birds, plus camel rides.
Rte FV2, La Lajita. Tel: 928 161 135. Open: daily 9am–6pm.
La Rosita Camels are still used to pull ploughs and also give rides through the farm.

*Rte FV101, north of Villaverde, 3km
(1¾ miles) south of the FV109 junction.
Open: Mon–Sat 10am–6pm.*
Oceanarium Explorer Sea creatures in
'touch tanks', and viewed from
underwater in a submarine.
*Puerto Castillo yacht harbour.
Tel: 928 163 514. Open: daily sailings
10.30am–4.30pm.*

Sailing ships
Lanzarote
*Marea Errota. Playa Blanca harbour.
Tel: 928 517 633, 676 965 403.
www.mareaerrota.com. Sails: Tue–Fri
10.45am–3.45pm.*

Fuerteventura
Pedra Santaña. Pirate-themed cruises.
*Port of Morro Jable. Tel (mobile):
670 745 5191. Sails: Mon–Sat.*

Waterparks
Lanzarote
Aquapark Waterslides, swimming pools
and playgrounds.
*Avda. de Teguise, Costa Teguise.
Tel: 928 592 128. Open: daily 10am–6pm.*

Fuerteventura
Baku Water Park Eight waterslides and
a wave pool.
*Avda. de Canarias, Corralejo.
Tel: 928 867 227. Open: daily
Apr–Oct 10am–6pm.*

Whales
Kids will be fascinated to walk around a
whale skeleton.

There's a complete whale skeleton at
Puerto Calero, Lanzarote, and at Las
Salinas, just south of Caleta de Fuste on
Fuerteventura, there's one on the beach
at the Museo de Sal.

Windmills
Children may be surprised to learn
how many windmills there are in the
Canary Islands.

Fuerteventura
Molino de Antigua A restored windmill
that children can go inside.
*Rte FV20, north of Antigua.
Tel: 928 878 041. Open: Tue–Fri & Sun
9.30am–5.30pm.*
Windmill Interpretive Centre The best
place to learn how they work.
*Rte FV20, Tiscamanita. Tel: 928 164 275.
Open: Tue–Fri & Sun 9.30am–5.30pm.*

Children are fascinated by the plants at Jardín
de Cactus

Sport and leisure

A temperate climate, warm crystal-clear waters, steady winds, long beaches and good surf all combine to make Lanzarote and Fuerteventura among the top water sports meccas for both amateurs and professionals.

The windy conditions attract experienced boardsailers, and make Fuerteventura one of the world's favourite windsurfing destinations. But there are plenty of sheltered bays where beginners can get instruction. While the water sports centres of Fuerteventura and Lanzarote get plenty of attention, land sports have not been as well developed. However short on supply, golf courses are of good quality, and the climate makes any outdoor sport a pleasure.

LAND SPORTS
Cycling
Mountain and street bikes are available for hire in all major resort areas.

Lanzarote
Bike Station Full range of bikes available. Rentals include helmet, pump and water bottle; child seats available for €1. Rentals from €11/day, €49/week. *Centro Comercial Maretas (near the post office), Costa Teguise. Tel: 628 102 177.*

Open: Mon–Fri 9.30am–12.30pm & 5.30–6.30pm, Sat–Sun 10–noon & 6–7pm.
Famara Surf Rental of mountain bikes. *Avda. Marinero. Tel: 928 528 676. www.famarasurf.com*
Renner Bikes Children's bikes, 7-gear and 21-gear suspension bikes can be hired by the day (from €10/day) or week (from €49/week). Prices include helmet, lock, tube, pump, bottle and child carrier. Free pick-up service. *Centro Comercial Marítimo (upper floor), Avda. de las Playas, Puerto del Carmen. Tel: 928 510 612, mobile: 629 990 755. www.mountainbike-lanzarote.com*

Fuerteventura
Vulcano Biking *Calle Acorazado España, Corralejo. Tel: 928 535 706.*

Golf
There is still a dearth of clubs on the islands, but quality is good. The following have a driving range, practice

putting green, club and trolley hire, and clubhouse.

Lanzarote

Club de Golf Costa Teguise Handicap required: 28 men, 32 women. 18-hole, par-72 course; lessons available. *Avda. de Golf, Costa Teguise. Tel: 928 590 512. www.lanzarote-golf.com*

Fuerteventura

Fuerteventura Golf Club 18-hole par-71 course, set in a hotel complex with modern facilities. *Off FV2, 0.5km (1/3 mile) south of Caleta de Fuste. Tel: 928 163 922.*

Tennis

Many larger hotels have tennis courts for their guests, which are hired out to the public as well. In Lanzarote facilities are available at Club La Santa, near Tinajo. *Tel: 928 840 101.*

SPECTATOR SPORTS
Wrestling
(*Lucha Canaria*)

This traditional fighting sport is likely to appeal to fans of Sumo wrestling

or Cumberland or Westmorland wrestling. The basic objective is to throw your opponent to the ground, but there are other rituals to be observed. The sport is active on all the islands, and most villages have a team comprising 12 wrestlers. Many

communities have an arena; look for posters announcing matches during your stay.

WATER SPORTS
Big-game fishing

Lanzarote Fishing operates four boats out of Puerto del Carmen, all perfect for open ocean

Windsurfers on Fuerteventura

trolling for the likes of marlin, tuna, wahoo and shark, or bottom fishing for some of the succulent local fish. The six-hour trips include bait, tackle, lunch and pick-up.

Puerto del Carmen harbour. Tel: 928 514 322, 629 731 293. http://lanzarotefishing.viviti.com Sails: 8.30am.

Blue Nose

All tackle is provided.
Puerto del Morro Jable. Tel: (628) 021 451. Sails: daily 8am–3pm for deep-sea fishing or 9am–2pm for rod fishing.

Deep-sea fishing

Shark, barracuda, swordfish, sailfish, marlin, tuna and even stingray are all on the big-game menu for the fishermen who set out from the many marinas on the islands. A stop at any marina in the afternoon as boats return will show which have the most success, as proud fishermen pose with their catch. The principal charter marinas on Fuerteventura are Caleta de Fuste and Gran Tarajal, and on Lanzarote most are at Playa Blanca and Puerto Calero.

La Caleta de Famara surf shop

Diving

Diving is very popular in the Canary Islands because of the warm, clear waters. Marine life, wrecks and reefs are not as prolific here as in other more exotic diving destinations in the world, but underwater parks have been designated off both the north and south coasts of Fuerteventura and the north coast of Lanzarote. The island of La Graciosa and the coast off Caleta de Fuste are among the favourite dive sites. The islands' geographic position attracts migratory species, resulting in a great variety of sea life, and the water is exceedingly clear.
All the following clubs give instruction.

Lanzarote
Aquatis Diving Centre
Equipment hire, guided excursions and instruction, with both shore and boat dives. PADI and RSTC.
Playa de las Cucharas and Hotel Zocos, Costa Teguise. Tel: 928 590 407. Also at Hotel Beatriz

Playa, Puerto del Carmen.
Tel: 928 590 407.
www.diving-lanzarote.net
**Cala Blanca Diving
Centre** Hire and sales of
diving and snorkel
equipment, guided
diving excursions. PADI
and BSAC.
*El Papagayo Shopping
Centre, Playa Blanca. Tel:
928 519 040, 607 301 230.
www.calablancasub.com*
Calipso Diving Guided
excursions and
instruction. PADI
and BSAC.
*Centro Comercial
Náuticol, Avda. de las Islas
Canarias, Costa Teguise.
Tel: 928 590 879.
www.calipso-diving.com*

Diving Lanzarote
Equipment hire, guided
excursions and a full
range of instruction.
PADI and CMAS.
*Puerto Calero, Yaiza.
Tel: 928 511 880.
www.divelanzarote.com*
M A Scuba Diving
*Calle Juan Carlos I,
Puerto del Carmen.
Tel: 928 516 915.
www.madiving.com*

Fuerteventura
Deep Blue Year-round
diving excursions and
instruction, with
beginners' courses
and PADI.
*Barcelo Club El Castillo,
Caleta de Fuste.*

*Tel: 928 163 712,
606 275 468.
www.deep-blue-
diving.com*
Dive Center Corralejo
This school and centre
offers lessons at all levels,
from beginners to
assistant instructors.
Using about 40 sites,
including Los Lobos,
they provide guided and
unguided trips as well
as snorkelling.
*Nuestra Señora del Pino
22. Tel: 928 535 906. www.
divecentercorralejo.com*
Felix Club Reef dives
twice daily for
experienced divers.
*Jandía.
Tel: 928 541 418.*

Surfing at Playa de Ojos

Punta Amanay, Diving Centre and Resort The PADI-qualified scuba-diving school is located at the end of the ferry dock. The simplest course is 'Try Diving', which includes a theory lesson, a pool lesson and one open water dive for only €65. The open water diver course (5 lessons, pool and 4 open water dives) is €360. More experienced divers can arrange boat and gear hire.
Calle El Pulpo 5, Corralejo.
Tel: 928 535 357, mobile: 656 447 657.
www.punta-amanay.com

Sailing

Boats of various sizes can be hired from sports marinas (*puertos deportivos*) around the islands. Below are some of the principal marinas, local sailing clubs and federations.

Lanzarote
Marina office, Puerto Calero. Tel: 928 814 437.

Fuerteventura
Aldiana Yacht Club
Carretera de Jandía,

Jandía. Tel: 928 541 147/48.

Cat Company Hires out catamarans by the hour and teaches courses at all levels. The sheltered beach is good for inexperienced sailors.
Grand Resort, Las Playitas.
Tel: 928 161 376, mobile: 616 619 313.
www.catamaran-segeln.de/en/kontakt.php. Open: daily 10am–6pm.

Snorkelling
Fuerte Snorkelling
Trips from Corralejo to the maritime reserves of Isla de Lobos across the bay take a maximum of eight persons per trip, leaving at 10am and 1pm daily.
Tel: 680 856 122.
www.fuerteservices.com

Surfing
There is little organised surfing on the islands. It's normally the locals who brave dangerous seas and currents, or the experienced professional. That said, the islands do have some outstanding training centres, where beginners can learn from

the best and more experienced surfers can improve their skills. The best locations on Fuerteventura include Isla de Lobos and beaches around Corralejo and El Cotillo. On Lanzarote the best spots are Playa Famara and La Santa. Never surf alone.

Lanzarote
Calima Surf Camps
Week-long or daily classes in surfing.
Calle Achique 14, La Caleta de Famara.
Tel: 626 913 369.
www.calimasurf.com

Fuerteventura
Quiksilver Surf School
Professionally taught courses include insurance, equipment, meals, lodging and transportation.
Calle Anzuelo, Corralejo.
Tel: 928 867 307. www.quiksilver-surfschool.com. Closed: Sun.
Red Shark Kite and surf camps and courses.
Calle Anzuelo, Corralejo.
Tel: 928 867 548. www.redsharkfuerteventura.com. Open: Mon–Sat 10am–1.30pm & 5–9pm.

Waterskiing

Although not as popular as other water sports, waterskiing is available on Fuerteventura at Corralejo Beach, and on Lanzarote at Puerto del Carmen's Fariones Beach, as well as in Playa Blanca at Los Delfines Watersports, and at Playa Dorada, next to Hotel Playa Dorada. See also **Lanzarote Surf Company**, *Playa Las Cucharas, Costa Teguise. Tel: 928 346 022.*

Windsurfing

Windsurfing is very popular, and is practised off almost any beach. Among the most popular are: Puerto del Carmen, Los Fariones, Playa de los Pocillos and Playa de Matagorda. The following are only the main centres, where lessons are available, usually located right on the beach. (*See pp132–3.*)

Lanzarote
Surf School Lanzarote
Carries the British Surfing Association's highest award (the BSA Level 4). *La Caleta de Famara.*

Tel: 928 528 623, 686 004 909. www. surfschoolanzarote.com
Windsurf Paradise Lanzarote Equipment hire, lessons, excursions. *Calle la Corvina 8, Costa Teguise. Tel: 928 346 022. www. windsurflanzarote.com*
Windsurfing Club Hirings, plus instruction for all levels. *Calle Las Olas 18, Costa Teguise. Tel: 928 590 731. www. sportaway-lanzarote.com*

Fuerteventura
Bahía Sports *Mancha 20, Jandía. Tel: 928 532 226.*
Fanatic Fun Centre *Playa de Costa Calma,*

Hotel Monica beach, Costa Calma. Tel: 928 535 999, 659 552 408.
Fanatic Surf Centre *Caleta de Fuste. Tel: 928 866 486.*
Flag Beach Windsurf Centre *Corralejo. Tel: 928 866 389, UK 0871 711 5036. www.flagbeach.com. Open: daily in summer 9am–7pm, winter 9.30am–5pm.*
Pro Centre *Los Gorriones Hotel, Playa Barca, Jandía. Tel: 606 360 297.*
Robinson Club *Playa del Matorral, Jandía. Tel: 928 168 000.*
Ventura Surf *Corralejo. Tel: 928 866 295.*

Windsurfing off Corralejo

Food and drink

Canarian food is tasty and fresh, though rarely either pretentious or elegantly presented. Unfortunately, in the tourist centres it's easier to find an Irish pub or a 'full English breakfast' than a Canarian típico (typical native restaurant). The latter's menu usually lists soups, stews and plenty of grilled fish dishes, along with generous starter salads.

Canarian cuisine

Canarian cuisine is essentially peasant and fishermen's food, and the meats most often used include pork, goat, chicken and rabbit.

Soups and stews are the most typical Canarian meals. *Potaje* has only vegetables; add meat to make *rancho canario*, and add more meat still to make *puchero*. The most popular seasonings include thyme, marjoram, parsley, cumin and coriander. A Guanche staple, *gofio* (maize meal), once eaten as bread, is still used to thicken stews. Another common stew is *garbanzo compuesto* (chickpea stew with meat), often available as a starter.

The fishing tradition of the islands gives local chefs a head start with fish, so those who love seafood will be in food heaven here. Fresh fish is always on the menu, which may offer a bewildering assortment whose names are untranslatable. If in doubt, ask to see the fish. These are most often served

fried or grilled, and, in general, local chefs are at their very best with grilled white fish, although shrimps and mussels are also excellent.

As an accompaniment you will be served *papas arrugadas* ('wrinkled potatoes'), which you can also get as a starter. These are small potatoes, boiled in their skins in very salty water. Until you taste these with a touch of *mojo*, it is hard to imagine the lowly potato raised to such delectable heights. On the table there will be two cold olive oil-based sauces: red *mojo picón* (piquant sauce) and *mojo verde* (green sauce). The latter is a tasty garlic, parsley and coriander sauce, perfect with fish; the former is a spicy garlic, chilli and paprika mix, and either one is excellent with the *papas*.

Do try the local cheese, wherever you are (*see pp108–9*). This is always made from goats' milk, and either fresh or aged it is invariably good. It is frequently a component of the Canarian salad.

Fish-eating vegetarians will find abundant seafood choices, but vegans will not find special menus.

Drinks

Lanzarote is famous for Malvasia-style wines, grown on the volcanic soil. These come in dry as well as sweet styles, and are good-quality table wines, rich and full-bodied. Bottled local wines are inexpensive, and the house wine, *vino de casa*, may be quite good. It is always acceptable to ask for a small sample of the house wine before ordering it. Canarian after-dinner drinks include *mistel* (a sweet wine) and *parra* (aguardiente brandy). *Ronmiel* (rum-honey) is found everywhere.

SANCOCHO

This is a popular dish with the Canarians, made up of herbs, salted fish, sweet potatoes, and vegetables, all cooked together.

PAPAS ARRUGADAS

(Wrinkled potatoes) Small potatoes in their skins are boiled with rock salt (a lot) and then served with *mojo* (a hot paprika and chilli sauce) to dip them in.

Restaurant at Casa Santa María, Betancuria

Food and drink

WHERE TO EAT

Restaurant dining is relatively inexpensive, except in the most de luxe resorts, and even there only in their top-end restaurants. Competition tends to keep prices down in resorts, and in the villages restaurants are priced for locals. If you don't mind fairly basic amenities and a menu with little choice, and you can manage a little Spanish, the latter is nearly always better value and more enjoyable than a resort eatery filled with holidaymakers. Portions are usually large, and often the generous starters – a typical Canarian soup-stew or a serving of mussels – are plenty for a main course. The giant Canarian salads featuring cheese, vegetables and tuna on a bed of greens are ample for a light meal or lunch. As a starter, consider ordering one of these for two people to share (*'vamos a compartir'*).

Be sure to ask the price of the daily fish specials, since if they are a hard-to-find variety, they can often cost considerably more than the regular menu items.

In the listings below, the average cost of a three-course meal, per person, with a half-bottle of wine or a couple of beers, is indicated by the following symbols:

★   €10.50–15
★★   €15–20
★★★   €20–50

FUERTEVENTURA
Ajuy
Casa Pepin, Puerto la Peña Restaurant ★
Uphill from the harbour, good food and friendly local feeling.

Antigua
La Flor de Antigua ★★
Pleasant dining experience with a Canarian flair.
Carretera del Valle 43. Tel: 928 878 168. Open: noon–4pm & 6–11pm daily.
El Molino ★★
Updated Fuerteventuran specialities, such as

El Chupa restaurant in La Geria

corvina fish in white wine sauce, are served in an atmospheric former granary building.
Carretera del Sur, km19. Tel: 928 878 220.

Betancuria
Casa Santa María ★★
In a traditional home with fine wood ceilings, serving chops of kid and leg of lamb.
Plaza Santa María. Tel: 928 878 282. Open: noon–7pm (summer); 11am–6pm (winter).

Caleta de Fuste
Los Caracolitos ★
Family-owned seafood restaurant, on the beach at Las Salinas, with transport to hotels.
Las Salinas del Carmen, Tel: 928 174 242. Open: Mon–Fri noon–9pm, Sat noon–6pm.

Tommy Nutters ★
English food and drink are what this bar and restaurant are all about. Full English breakfasts, Sunday roasts, ribs, bangers and beers are served by friendly hosts, who also act as a source of reliable information for visitors. No credit cards.

Downstairs at Castillo Central under the Mexican Corner. Tel: 619 476 597. Open: daily 9am–midnight.

Restaurante Frasquita ★★
Seafood specialities, overlooking the beach and marina.
Aulaga 20, at the end of the beach. Tel: 928 163 657. Open: Tue–Sun 1–4pm & 6–10pm.

Corralejo
La Ola, Panadería Artesanía ★
A perfect place for breakfast and lunch, this German-style bakery overlooks the ferry harbour and serves pastries, croissants, breads and sandwiches.
Paseo Marítimo Bristol. Tel: 928 535 304.

La Marquesina ★★
Locals and tourists mix in this busy seafood restaurant. Serves great fish in a salt crust.
Muelle Viejo, in the old town. Tel: 928 535 435. Open: daily 11am–11pm.

Mesón Canario Tío Bernabé ★★–★★★
The food is well prepared but a bit slow in this popular restaurant with

a lively atmosphere. Watch live traditional Canarian music. Make sure you ask the price of specials.
Calle La Iglesia 17. Tel: 928 535 895. Open: noon–midnight.

La Scarpetta ★★★
Beautiful fresh pasta. Italian food for hedonists accompanied by incredible dynamic and organic wines.
Calle Juan de Austria, Centro Comercial La Menara. Tel: 928 535 887, 660 101 275.

El Cotillo
Azzuro Restaurante ★★
Specialities of this attractive restaurant on the road to the lighthouse are fresh meats and fish and pasta plus a nice selection of wines, including those from Lanzarote.
Carretera al Faro. Tel: 928 175 360. Open: Tue–Sun for lunch & dinner.

Casa Rustica ★★
A bit more international in style but with a local touch. Well-prepared food, good international wine selection.

Calle Constitución 1.
Tel: 928 538 728.
Roque de los Pescadores ★★
Fish dishes are excellent, as are generous salads, plates of local cheese, avocados and shrimp. The terrace overlooks the little fishing harbour.
Tel: 928 538 713. Open: daily 11am–11pm.

La Ampuyenta
Fabiola ★★★
French cuisine in a most unusual space that cocoons you. An oasis in the middle of this desert island. Local architecture and European chic. Don't miss their chocolate cake.
Tel: 928 174 605.
Book in advance.

Lajares
Los Pinchitos ★
In the centre of town, this lovely humble bar serves the best homemade traditional food. Do not miss the carne mechada con papas fritas and the fried octopus. For desserts we recommend you cross over to El Goloso Bakery.
Tel: 928 868 181.
Closed: Wed.

Pizzería La Cancela ★
This is a good stop for lunch, offering tasty pizza, pasta dishes and a selection of traditional tapas.
Calle Central 2.
Tel: 928 868 568. Open: Wed–Mon 5–11pm.

La Lajita
Restaurante Ramón ★
Facing the beach with good views of the headland. The speciality is fish, nicely prepared.
Tel: 928 872 126.

Los Molinos
Restaurante Casa Pon ★
Popular with locals, serving fresh fish, paella and Canarian-style tapas.
Open: Mon–Fri 10am–6pm, Sat 10am–7pm, Sun 10am–10pm.

Pájara
Casa Isaítas ★★
Beautiful personalised dishes made using locally produced, seasonal ingredients.
Calle Guize 7 (opposite the public car park).
Tel: 928 161 402, 607 928 307.
www.casaisaitas.com

Pozo Negro
Los Pescadores ★★
Seafood, as you would expect from the name (which means the fishermen) and location.
On the beach.
Tel: 928 174 653.

Puerto del Rosario
La Saranda Meso-Cafetería ★
On the main business street near Iglesia de la Virgen del Rosario, this bright non-smoking café serves breakfast (with freshly squeezed juices), sandwiches and light meals.
Calle Primero de Mayo 46. Tel: 928 530 330.
Hotel Fuerteventura Playa Blanca ★★
Canarian and Spanish entrées prevail in this attractive former parador dining room.
Playa Blanca 45 (near the airport).
Tel: 928 851 150.

Vega del Río Palma
Restaurante Don Antonio ★★★
One of the best on the island, using fresh local ingredients. Very upmarket.

*Tel: 928 878 757.
www.lanzarote-
fuerte.com/donantonio.
Open: Tue–Sun.*

Villaverde
**Restaurante El
Horno ★★**
Traditional Canarian
food, with a speciality in
grilled meats, served in a
rustic country setting.
*Carretera General 191.
Tel: 928 868 671.
Open: Tue–Sat 12.30–
11pm, Sun 12.30–4.30pm.*
Restaurante Mahoh ★★
Canarian dishes are
the speciality, with
Sunday menus that
include roast suckling
pig, roasted kid,
traditional stews and
mixed paellas.
*Sitio de Juan Bello.
Tel: 928 868 050. Open:
Thur–Tue 1pm–midnight.*
Casa Marcos ★★★
Tucked away in a
traditional-style building,
this family place
specialises in tapas
including belotta ham
(from the finest acorn-
fed hogs) and goats'
cheeses of the island.
A fine wine cellar.
*Carretera General 94.
Tel: 928 868 285.*

*Open: Thur–Tue noon–
4pm & 7.30–11.30pm
(until midnight, Fri–Sat),
closed Sun for lunch.*

LANZAROTE
Arrecife
Leito de Proa ★
Bar and restaurant beside
the waters of El Charco.
Very popular with locals.
*Tel: 928 802 066.
Open: daily noon–4.30pm
& 7–11pm.*
Casa Ginori ★★
Simple but highly
recommended restaurant
that overlooks the fort on
Puerto Naos. Try the
'marriage' dish.

*Calle Juan de Quesada 9.
Tel: 928 804 045.
Closed: Sun.*
**Restaurante Castillo de
San José ★★★**
Fine dining in a
Manrique-designed
restaurant, at the castle
that houses the Museo de
Arte Contemporáneo.
Suitable clothing
required; no shorts.
*Castillo de San José, Avda.
de Naos. Tel: 928 812 321.
Open: 1–11pm.*

La Caleta de Famara
Restaurante El Risco ★★
Windows over the sea;
known for fresh seafood

The climate makes dining outdoors a perfect option

and a collection of Manrique paintings.
Calle Montaña Blanca. Tel: 928 528 550. Open: Fri–Wed.

Costa Teguise

Restaurante Masil ★
Good seafood and local dishes.
Calle Las Olas. Tel: 928 590 143.

La Jordana ★★
One of Teguise's best restaurants, in Playa Bastian. Folksy country style décor. High-quality international cooking.
Calle Los Geranios 1. Tel: 928 590 328. Open: Mon–Sat noon–4pm & 6–11pm, closed Sun.

Neptuno Restaurant ★★
Roast lamb and seafood in pleasant, bright surroundings.
Avda. del Jablillo, Centro Comercial Neptuno. Tel: 928 590 378. Open: Mon–Sat 1–4pm & 7pm– midnight, closed Sun.

Portobello ★★
Excellent food and service in this restaurant at Las Cucharas Beach.
Centro Comercial Las Cucharas. Tel: 928 590 241. Open: Tue–Sun 1–11.30pm, closed Mon.

Patio Canario ★★–★★★
Impeccably fresh local fish, lovingly prepared. Ask about the daily fish specials. Rodaballo is a local flounder-type fish.
Puerto Marinero. Tel: 928 346 234. Open: daily, lunch & dinner.

La Chimenea ★★★
Elegant beachside dining and international menu.
Avda. Islas Canarias. Tel: 928 590 837. Open: Mon–Sat, closed July.

El Golfo

Mar Azul Restaurant ★
A friendly local restaurant, specialising in fish and seafood.
Avda. del Golfo 42. Tel: 928 173 132. Open: daily 11am–10pm.

Mirador Salinas Casa Domingo ★–★★
High above the Salinas de Janubio, with fine views of the multicoloured saltpans.
Salinas de Janubio. Tel: 928 173 070.

Haría

Restaurante Dos Hermanos ★
Serves typical traditional Canarian dishes, such as

rabbit, fried goat, mussels and limpets. Indoor and outdoor dining.
Plaza de León y Castillo. Tel: 928 835 409. www.optillave.com/dosher manos. Open: daily 11am–8pm.

Restaurante Los Helechos ★
Before beginning the descent into Haría you might want to stop here. It is at the Mirador overlooking the sea and Haría. Good and inexpensive food served cafeteria-style.
Mirador de Montaña de Haría. Tel: 928 835 089. Open: daily 10.30am– 6.30pm.

Restaurante Cafetería Ney-Ya ★–★★
Specialities of tapas and traditional Canarian dishes.
Plaza Constitución. Tel: 928 835 409. Open: lunch and dinner.

Puerta Verde ★★
International dishes served in a pleasant informal atmosphere.
Calle Fajardo 20. Tel: 620 347 644. Open: Wed–Sat 11am–9pm.

Mala

Bar Restaurante Don Quijote ★

On the road between Arrieta and Guatiza near the Jardín de Cactus, this makes a conveniently situated lunch stop or tapas break. Serves Mediterranean dishes as well as vegetarian food. *El Rostro 1.*

Tel: 928 529 301. Open: Thur–Tue noon–11pm.

Montaña de Fuego

El Diablo ★★

All the cooking is done on the grill above the live volcano. Superb views. *Islote del Hilario, Parque Nacional de Timanfaya. Tel: 928 173 105. Open: daily noon–3.30pm.*

Mozaga

Caserío de Mozaga ★★

Fine dining in a country finca atmosphere, at the Hotel Rural. *Calle Mozaga 8. Tel: 928 520 060. www. caseriodemozaga.com. Open: Mon–Thur & Sat 7.30–10.30pm, Fri & Sun 1–4pm & 7.30–10.30pm.*

Food and drink

Get a taste for the local specialities

Nazaret (near Teguise)

Restaurante Lagomar ★★★

Fine dining in an ex-holiday villa of Omar Sharif. Specialises in Basque dishes; also holds art exhibitions.

Los Loros 6.
Tel: 928 845 665. Open:
Tue–Sat noon–midnight.

Orzola

La Perla del Atlántico ★★

Seafood and fish are the speciality, well prepared and nicely presented.

Calle Peña Sr Dionisio 1.
Tel: 928 842 589.
Open: 10am–6pm.

Restaurante El Norte ★★

Specialises in fresh fish, but with a full range of other dishes.

Calle Embarcadero 6.
Tel: 928 842 590.
Open: 10am–6pm.

Playa Blanca

El Almacén de la Sal ★★

Specialises in fish and Basque dishes, served on a terrace with a sea view.

Avda. Marítima 12.
Tel: 928 517 885.
www.almacendelasal.com

Playa Quemada

7 Islas ★–★★

Set into the hillside above this tiny south-coast fishing village, the restaurant serves good fish and salad plates. If the thermals are right you can watch paragliders launching from a nearby hill.

Playa Quemada.
Tel: 928 173 249.
Open: daily noon–9pm.

Puerto Calero

Café La Parisienne ★

Occupying the prime corner of the promenade, the café serves ice creams, a choice of teas, sandwiches and daily lunch specials.

Open: Mon–Fri from 8am,
Sat–Sun from 8.30am.

Puerto del Carmen

El Balandro ★★

Located uphill, away from the busy harbour, near Apartamentos Balcón del Mar and Flora, this is a nice place for dinner. The veal is splendid and the fish well prepared.

Avda. Reina Sofía 29.
Tel: 928 510 894.
Open: Tue–Sun lunch
& dinner.

La Bodega Tapas Bar ★★

Tapas, mainland dishes; Spanish guitar trio.

Calle Roque Nublo 5.
Tel: 928 512 953.
Open: 1pm–midnight.

El Bodegón ★★

Tapas in a winery atmosphere; local and Spanish dishes.

Avda. del Varadero.
Tel: 928 515 265.

Restaurante Puerto Bahía ★★

On the promenade where the cliffs overlook the harbour and the sea, this is a romantic place to dine. The food is good and the views splendid, or stop for a glass of wine and tapas as the sun sets.

Avda. del Varadero 5.
Tel: 928 513 793. Open:
daily 10am–midnight.

El Sardinero Restaurante Bodegón ★★

Pavement tables sit at the centre of activity, and the food is excellent. If they offer a special of salt baked fish, do order it. Grilled sardines are served at lunch only.

Calle Tenerife–El Varadero.
Tel: 928 512 128.
Open: daily 11am–11pm.

La Dolce Vita

Due ★★–★★★

The terrace overlooks the port and kids' football pitch, the favourite promenade in the evening, with good people-watching. The chef substitutes pork in several traditional Italian veal dishes.

Nuestra Señora del Carmen. Tel: 928 511 161. Open: daily 5–11.30pm.

Tahiche

El Pastelito ★

German-style bakery and café, the perfect place for a sandwich or a pastry.

Avda. Nestor de la Torre 22. Tel: 928 843 316. Open: Tue–Fri 8am–7pm, Sat–Sun 8am–8pm, closed Mon.

Teguise (see also Nazaret)

Bar Cafetería Tahona ★

The clientele are mostly locals, enjoying well-prepared local specialities, big servings. Live guitar music Friday evenings. On Sunday (market day) get there before 1.30pm.

Calle Santo Domingo. Open: daily.

Patio del Vino ★

Tapas, in the courtyard of the Palacio del Marqués.

Calle Herrera y Rojas 9. Tel: 928 845 773, 609 475 043. Open: Mon–Fri noon–8pm, Sun 10am–3pm, closed Sat.

Casa Suso 8 ★–★★

A pleasant traditional restaurant well located on the main road, serving international and Canarian entrées.

Corner of Calle Gran Aldea 62 & Tazacorte 1. Tel: 928 845 925. Open: daily lunch & dinner; very busy on Sundays.

Restaurante Acatife ★★

Fine Canarian and Spanish specialities are served in a historic setting.

Calle San Miguel 4, Plaza de la Constitución. Tel: 928 845 037. Open: Tue–Sun noon–11pm.

Tiagua

Mesón Tiagua ★★

Innovative international specialities using native Canarian products, served in a setting of open-beam ceilings and traditional art.

Avda. Guanarteme 12. Tel: 928 529 816. Open:

Mon–Sat 7–11pm, Sun 1–4pm & 7–11pm.

Yaiza

El Chupadero Finca & Bodega ★–★★

The perfect place for a glass of wine or tapas while exploring La Geria.

Rte LZ30, 4km (2½ miles) from Uga. Tel: 928 173 115. www.el-chupadero.com. Open: Tue–Sun.

La Era ★★★

Fine Canarian food in a splendid manor house. It escaped the 1730 volcanoes, to be restored by Manrique in 1968.

El Barranco 3. Tel: 928 830 016. Open: Tue–Sun 1–11pm.

Yé

Bodega Volcán de la Corona ★

Dining and wine sales at an old winery.

Rte LZ10, near the turn to Mirador del Río.

Yé Cultural Centre ★

In the centre of the tiny village you can get a freshly made sandwich and drinks, while enjoying the murals.

Accommodation

The vast majority of accommodation here has been built over the last 20 years to cater for package holidaymakers, with holiday communities mostly concentrated in the large resorts. Unfortunately for independent travellers, there is no tradition of private accommodation nor the small type of family-run hotels that are found in mainland Spain. Look in the older resorts, the two capitals and the occasional seaside village to find 'unpackaged' accommodation.

Hotels

Any holiday brochure shows page upon page of characterless Canarian hotels, all built to a similar 3- or 4-star standard. These provide comfortable, well-equipped rooms, a swimming pool, bars, and perhaps sports facilities and boutiques. Many are large (around 300 rooms), and a good number have been redecorated and upgraded.

Travellers putting together their own package in 3- or 4-star hotels (or apartments) should shop around for prices. The hotels' stated nightly rates often bear little resemblance to what may be found online. In general, however, it would be difficult to beat the price of a late-availability package.

Aparthotels

Featuring rooms with their own kitchen facilities, yet with the other trappings of an ordinary hotel, these are a good bet for families with children. Like hotels, they are not all well-run establishments, so it pays to

get as much advance information as possible. A very useful website for learning other travellers' recent experiences is *www.holidays-uncovered.co.uk*

Self-catering

Self-catering bungalows and apartments are especially popular here, and are usually grouped together in developments known as *urbanizaciones*. Caleta de Fuste, Corralejo and Puerto del Carmen have an excellent variety of these. They also often include timeshare apartments.

Casas rurales

Usually located in fine old fincas, these are among the few independent hotels on the islands, and are also one of the more expensive choices. But the experience of staying in a private country inn, far from the often madding crowds, gives a very different experience of the islands. Full or half board is usually available, and the food is often excellent.

Camping

Given the ideal climate for camping, sites are surprisingly few. There are very few official sites, but *camping sauvage* (wild camping) is tolerated in many places: enquire at the local tourist office. Camping sites are usually little more than treeless car parks where caravans may pull into spaces hardly bigger than their wheelbase. Just past Playa Papagayo, on Lanzarote, is the largest of these, and there is a much smaller – but equally bare – one at Pozo Negro, on Fuerteventura.

Timeshare

Although you will hear much about the annoyance of timeshare touts on the Canary Islands, they are not especially common on these two islands. The two golden rules are: never sign anything while on holiday (go home and 'cool off' first), or without sound legal advice.

Youth hostels

There is one youth hostel on Fuerteventura.

Albergue Pozo Negro, Pozo Negro. *Tel: 928 174 666, (696) 995 794, fax: 928 878 200.*

Prices

Ratings are for a double room per night:
- ★ under €50
- ★★ €50–100
- ★★★ over €100

Balcón del Mar in Puerto del Carmen

FUERTEVENTURA
Antigua
Era de la Corte ★★★
An attractive, characterful hotel. All 11 rooms have full bath, TV and phone, in a fully restored 1890 family home. Pool, solarium, tennis, bicycles, garden and restaurant.
Calle La Corte 1. Tel: 928 878 705, fax: 928 878 710. Email: eradelacorte@ terra.es. www.eradelacorte.com

Caleta de Fuste
Barcelo Club El Castillo ★★
The complex includes spacious bungalows set in gardens, several restaurants, recreation and pool areas and frontage on one of the island's few good beaches for children.
Avda. José Franch y Roca, at the ocean end of Avda. del Castillo. Tel: 928 163 100, fax: 928 163 042. www.barcelo.com

Corralejo
Blue Bay Palace ★★★
One of the best hotels in Fuerteventura and in the Canary Islands according to customer ratings. Four-star plus, with top service.
Avda. Grandes Playas 12. Tel: 928 536 050. www.bluebayresorts.com

Puerto del Rosario
Hotel Fuerteventura Playa Blanca ★★
Former parador, in an attractive beachside building.
Calle Playa Blanca 45. Tel: 928 851 150, fax: 928 851 158. Email: hotelfuerteventura@cabildofuer.es.

LANZAROTE
Arrecife
Hotel Miramar ★★
On the promenade, with 85 renovated and comfortable rooms, restaurant and café.
Avda. Coll 2. Tel: 928 812 600, fax: 928 801 533. www.hmiramar.com

Arrecife Gran Hotel ★★★
Modern, comfortable high-rise on the beach, with indoor parking.
Parque Islas Canarias. Tel: 928 800 000, fax: 928 805 906.
Email: info@arrecifehoteles.com. www.arrecifehoteles.com.

Costa Teguise
Gran Melia Salinas ★★★
If you are ever going to treat yourself to a 5-star experience, do it here. The soaring, tropical lobby atrium and public spaces were created by César Manrique, rooms are luxurious, pools magnificent and restaurants superb.
Avda. Islas Canarias. Tel: 928 590 040, fax: 928 590 390. Email: gran.melia.salinas@solmelia.com. www.solmelia.com.

Haría
Eckhoff B&B ★
One cosy, hospitable double room with private bath, terrace and use of the hot tub on the terrace. Dining area on a secluded balcony. English-speaking host. Minimum of two nights, but the rate is low enough that you could pay for two nights and use it for only one.
Calle Longuera 22. Tel: 928 835 761.

Mozaga (near San Bartolomé)
Hotel Rural El Caserío de Mozaga ★★–★★★
Attractive rural hotel, with private baths, TV and patio; breakfast and dinner available.
Calle Mozaga 8. Tel: 928 520 060, fax: 928 522 029.
www.caseriodemozaga.com

Playa Blanca
Atlantic Gardens Bungalows ★★
Well located, 800m (½ mile) from Playa Flamingo, with two tennis courts, two pools, children's pool, buffet restaurant and bar.
Urb. Montaña Roja, Parcela 42.
Tel: 928 517 555, fax: 928 517 646.
Hotel Casa del Embajador ★★★
On the promenade near the beach, with two tennis courts.
Calle La Tegala 56. Tel: 928 519 191, fax: 928 519 192.
Email: info@casadelembajador.com.
www.hotelcasadelembajador.com
Hotel Gran Melia Volcán Lanzarote ★★★
Like a small village, around a spectacular pool.
Urb. Castillo del Aguila. Tel: 928 519 185, fax: 928 519 132. Email:
gran.melia.volcan.lanzarote@solmelia.com
www.solmelia.com

Puerto del Carmen
Apartamentos Flora ★
Three different sizes of refurbished apartments in an attractive hilltop neighbourhood, with pool, nursery, playground, restaurant and café.
Calle Reina Sofía 25. Tel: 928 514 900, fax: 928 512 141. Email:
flora@thbhotels.com. www.thbhotels.com
Balcón del Mar ★
Attractive bungalows and apartments in a garden setting overlooking the sea, most with balconies or patios.
Reina Sofía 23. Tel: 928 513 725, fax: 928 511 117.
Email: reservas@balcondelmar.com.
www.balcondelmar.com

San Bartolomé
Finca de la Florida ★★
Fine quarters in a country *finca*, with plenty of entertainment available: gym, sauna, swimming pool, tennis, table tennis and bicycles. Breakfast included, and an on-site restaurant.
El Islote 90 (12km/7½ miles from Puerto del Carmen). Office:
Apartamentos Kon-Tiki, Calle Guanapay 5, Puerto del Carmen. Tel: 928 521 124, fax: 928 520 311. Email:
reserva@hotelfincadelaflorida.com.
www.hotelfincadelaflorida.com

Uga (near Yaiza)
El Chupadero Finca & Bodega ★★
Apartments at a classy wine *finca*, a good base for exploring La Geria and Timanfaya. The moderate weekly rate also includes car hire, making this a real bargain.
Rte LZ30, 4km (2½ miles) from Uga. Tel: 928 173 115.
www.el-chupadero.com

Practical guide

Arriving

Visitors from EU countries, the USA and Canada need only a passport to enter the Canary Islands. A residence permit or special visa is necessary for stays longer than 90 days.

By air

There are international airports on both Fuerteventura (*Tel: 928 860 500*) and Lanzarote (*Tel: 928 846 000*). All airports have taxis to meet interisland flights, although the wait may be a long one.

By boat

There are no regular cruise-liner services to the Canaries. From mainland Spain, ships sail from Cádiz to Santa Cruz de Tenerife, to Las Palmas on Gran Canaria, and to Arrecife on Lanzarote.

Camping

There are very few official campsites on either island, and they tend to be open areas with tiny delineated spaces more like car parks than tent pitches or caravan sites.

Children

Both islands are completely geared for family holidays, and within the major resorts you will find all the usual babycare products. Babysitters can be found for older children, and many resort hotels have specific children's activities and 'clubs'.

Climate

Although the Canary Islands are known for their temperate climate, Lanzarote and Fuerteventura are swept by steady trade winds that can make it quite cool, but for most of the winter they are pleasantly spring-like to North Europeans. Rainy spells can occur – especially in the winter – even on these two islands, which are noted for their dry, desert-like conditions. Summer sunshine is virtually guaranteed everywhere.

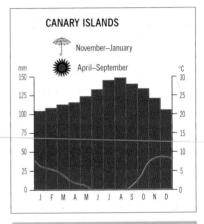

CANARY ISLANDS

November–January

April–September

WEATHER CONVERSION CHART

25.4mm = 1 inch

°F = 1.8 × °C + 32

Crime

Theft from cars is the most common form of crime against tourists on the islands, with handbag snatching an occasional second. Never leave anything

Some roads are suitable only for jeep safaris

the Canary Islands provide very reasonable car-hire rates, it hardly seems worth the effort or expense. Reliable and competitively priced local firms include the following:

Cicar Car Hire, a very good company with an office on every island: free phone from Spain *(900) 202 303*; from UK *0800 960 367*.

Top-Car Reisen has airport offices on Fuerteventura (*Tel: 928 860 760, fax: 928 860 762*) and in Lanzarote (*Tel: 928 846 255*).

Should you prefer to book from the UK, consult **Alamo** at *www.alamo.uk* or, in the USA, *www.alamo.com*, or **Hire for Lower**, *25 Savile Row, London W1X 1AA (tel: (020) 7491 1111)*.

Documentation

All British, European, American and Australian driving licences are valid, although it may be advisable to take a Spanish translation with you (contact a motoring organisation in your own country before travelling). An International Driving Permit is not necessary.

Petrol

Take cash, as many petrol stations do not accept credit cards. Stations are not in every town, but are marked on road maps. Be sure to begin any trip with a full tank if you plan to be away from the major towns or in the mountains. Don't expect 24-hour opening except in the larger resorts and towns.

of value visible in your car, and make sure it is locked at all times. Hotels usually have safes for hire, although staff members are honest and break-ins at good hotels are rare. Apartments are less easy to police. If you are a victim of robbery, report the incident to the local police who will give you a copy of your statement for insurance purposes.

Customs

For customs purposes the Canary Islands are not members of the EU. The duty-free allowance for goods taken in or out (applicable to people 17 and over) includes: 2 litres ($3^1/_2$pt) of wine; 1 litre ($1^3/_4$pt) of spirits; 200 cigarettes (or 100 cigarillos or 50 cigars or 250g (9oz) of tobacco); 60cc (2oz) of perfume or 250cc (9oz) of toilet water; £145-worth of gifts per person.

Driving
Car hire

It is possible to take your own car to the islands via mainland Spain, but as

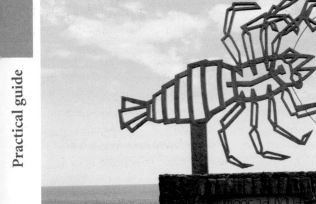

Jameos del Agua combines a natural wonder with the brilliance of Manrique

Rules of the road

Driving is on the right. Seat belts are compulsory in the front and the back, and children under 12 must travel in the back of the car. In towns, cars must be parked facing the direction of the movement of traffic. The standard of roads is surprisingly high, with many newly built and very smoothly surfaced. Watch out for sharp, high drop-offs in the paving at the verges; these can be dangerous. The standard of driving is quite reasonable, and drivers tend to be polite. Parking can be very difficult in resort towns. Beware the fiendish one-way system in Arrecife on Lanzarote.

Electricity

The current throughout the islands is 220 volts AC, and sockets take the circular two-pin continental-style plug.

Embassies and consulates

Embassies are located in Madrid. There are no consulates on either island; the nearest are on the two major islands, Tenerife and Gran Canaria. The following addresses are all consulates:

Ireland *Calle León y Castillo 195-1, Las Palmas, Gran Canaria. Tel: 928 297 728.*

UK *Edificio Cataluña, Calle de Luis Morote 6, 35007, Las Palmas, Gran Canaria. Tel: 928 262 508/262 658.*

USA *Calle Martínez de Escobar, 3 Las Palmas, Gran Canaria. Tel: 928 222 552. http://madrid.usembassy.gov*

Emergency telephone numbers

General: *112*
Police (all islands): *112*
Ambulance (Lanzarote): *112*

Ambulance (Fuerteventura): *112*
Fire Brigade (Lanzarote): *928 814 858*
Fire Brigade (Fuerteventura):
928 530 744

Health

No vaccinations are necessary for a visit to the Canary Islands.

You should take a European Health Insurance Card (EHIC) with you when you go; this can be obtained, free of charge, through most UK post offices or through the UK Department of Health via their website (*www.dh.gov.uk*) or by telephoning *0845 606 2030* (from outside the UK call *(0044) 19120 3555*). Medical insurance is still strongly advisable.

The most common complaints are stomach upsets caused by a sudden change of diet and too much sun. Break yourself in gradually to sunbathing, and always use suntan lotions and blocks. Remember that children are particularly vulnerable.

If you need to see a doctor, you will get good treatment from the local Social Security Community Health Centre. There are many English-speaking dentists and doctors. Ask your hotel or tourist information office for the nearest one.

Minor ailments can usually be treated at the chemist (*farmacia*). At least one chemist per town or area stays open after hours. Its location is posted in the window of all the other chemists.

Hitchhiking

This is legal, though not totally safe if you are alone, and with the large number of North European holiday drivers on the roads, not likely to be a quick way of getting around.

Lost property

Lost property offices are few and far between. Ask the tourist office where to go locally. Report lost valuables to the Municipal Police or Guardia Civil and obtain a form for your own holiday insurance purposes.

Maps

As new roads are built, so maps go out of date quite rapidly. Town plans and basic local maps are usually available from tourist offices.

The roads on Fuerteventura are well paved and smooth but lack bicycle lanes

International newspapers are available to buy on Lanzarote

Media

There are several newspapers and magazines written for the English-speaking visitor to the Canary Islands, and they are easy to find. Lanzarote offers the *Canary Island Gazette & Tourist Guide*. Free tourist magazines are generally available from tourist offices, travel agents, hotels and popular bars.

All the major international papers are available in the large towns and popular resorts, usually the day after publication.

Money matters

The euro (€) is the unit of currency used on the islands. There are seven denominations of the euro note: €5,

€10, €20, €50, €100, €200 and €500; eight denominations of coins: 1 cent, 2 cents, 5 cents, 10 cents, 20 cents, 50 cents, and €1 and €2. There is no limit to the amount of money you may bring onto the islands, but you are not allowed to take out more than €3,000.

By far the best way to convert currency is by using a bank credit or debit card at an ATM. These are located at most banks and are open 24 hours a day. Banks are open weekdays 9am to 2pm, 9am to 1pm on Saturdays (closed on Saturdays from 1 June to 31 October). A commission is always charged for changing money, and you will need your passport. Outside banking hours many travel agents and various bureaux de change (look for the *Cambio* sign) will exchange money, but always at a lower rate than the bank. Even if the rates on display seem attractive, the deductions which they fail to advertise will cost you dearly (tourist shops are the worst culprits). Most hotels will also change money for you.

If you need to transfer money quickly, you can use the MoneyGram[SM] Money Transfer service. For more details in the UK, telephone Freephone *0800 897198*.

Opening hours

In towns other than tourist resorts, shops are open Monday to Saturday, 9am–1pm and 4pm or 5pm to 7pm or 8pm (chemists usually close on Saturday afternoon except for the one duty chemist in each area, which is open 24 hours). In tourist areas, most shops stay open all day. Museum opening hours are variable; some close on Sunday, some on Saturday, others on a Monday (or occasionally another weekday), while some remain open all week. Church hours also vary, but they are often open for morning or evening services.

Places of worship

Catholic Mass is celebrated in various languages in the major resorts throughout the islands (details from the tourist office, the local newspapers, or on church notice boards).

There are Anglican services at Nuestra Señora de Carmen church at the old town harbour, Puerto del Carmen, on Lanzarote (Sunday 6pm).

Police

Police responsibilities are split between the Policía Municipal who direct traffic and have other municipal duties; the Policía Nacional who are in charge of crime in the towns; and the Guardia Civil who look after crime and patrol the highways in rural areas. For emergencies dial *112*.

Postal services

In large towns post offices are open weekdays 8.30am to 8.30pm, and 9.30am to 1pm on Saturday. There are no telephones in post offices.

Stamps (*sellos* or *timbres*) can also be bought at tobacconists, and from most shops that sell postcards. Postboxes are painted yellow. Use the slot marked *extranjeros* (foreign) for sending postcards home.

Public holidays

1 January New Year's Day
6 January Epiphany (*Reyes Magos*)
1 May Labour Day
15 August Assumption
12 October Columbus Day
1 November All Saints' Day
6 December Constitution Day
8 December Immaculate Conception
25 December Christmas Day
Moveable feasts are Maundy Thursday and Good Friday. In addition to these, there are several local feast days.

Public transport
Air

Binter Canarias, a subsidiary of the national airline, Iberia (*Tel: (London) (020) 7830 0011; www.bintercanarias.com*), runs regular flights between the islands. These are punctual and all flights are around 30 minutes. Enquire at any airport for a timetable or contact the local Binter offices (*Tel: (902) 391 392* for Fuerteventura and Lanzarote).

Ferries

Ferries run to all the islands, and hydrofoils or jetfoils run between both Tenerife and Gran Canaria to Fuerteventura, operated by **Compañía**

(*Cont. on p184*)

Language

Canarians speak Spanish, or to be more accurate Castilian (the language of most of mainland Spain). The only real difference that the non-language student will notice is that the letters **c** and **z** are pronounced softly, instead of lisped with a 'th' sound.

There are a few indigenous words still in use, the most notable being **papa(s)** for potato(es) and **guagua** (pronounced wah-wah) for bus.

It's quite possible in some major resorts to get through two weeks on the islands speaking, and even hearing, nothing but English. However, off the beaten track, and particularly on the smaller islands, a smattering of Spanish will be helpful if not essential. But wherever you are, your attempts to master a few phrases and, at the very least, daily greetings will always be appreciated.

Pronunciation

Try to remember the following basic rules:

Consonants

c is soft before e and i (eg, Barcelona), but hard at any other time – **como?** (pardon?) pronounced 'ko-mo'.

g at the start of a word is a hard sound (as in get). In the middle of a word it is like the throaty 'ch' as in the Scottish 'loch' – **urgencia** (emergency) is pronounced 'ooer-hensi-ah'. In **agua** (water) it is hardly pronounced at all ('ah-gwa').

h is always silent – **hospital** is pronounced 'ospitahl'.

j is also pronounced like the ch in 'loch' – **jamón** (ham) is pronounced 'ch-amon'.

ll is always like 'y' in 'yes' – **lleno** (full) is pronounced 'yay-no'.

ñ is like 'ni' in onion – **España** (Spain) is pronounced 'ay-spanya'.

qu is like k in key – **Cuánto?** (how much?) is pronounced 'kwan-toe'.

r is rolled: **rr** is rolled even harder.

v is pronounced like a 'b'.

x is like s – **excelente** (excellent) is pronounced 'ess-say-len-tay'.

Vowels

a is a short 'ah' sound – **gracias** (thank you). It is never long as in the English 'gracious'. All the other vowels are long sounds. The letter **e** is a cross between the short English e (as in get) and the long English a (as in grace) – **de** (of/from) is pronounced 'day' but in a clipped way. The letter **i** is a long 'ee' sound as in sí (yes), pronounced 'see', and **u** is like 'oo' in boot – **una** (one). The letter **o** is an 'oh' sound.

USEFUL WORDS AND PHRASES

yes/no	sí/no
hello	hola
good morning	buenos días
good afternoon	buenas tardes
goodnight	buenas noches
goodbye	adiós
please	por favor
thank you	gracias
you're welcome	de nada
today	hoy
tomorrow	mañana
yesterday	ayer
I am English	Soy inglés/inglesa
do you speak English?	¿habla inglés? (informal)
	¿habla Usted inglés? (formal)
very well/good	muy bien/vale
where is . . ?	¿dónde está . . ?
what/when	qué/cuándo
why/how	por qué/cómo
how much is . . ?	¿cuánto vale/cuesta . . ?
here/there	aquí/ahí
open/closed	abierto/cerrado
right	derecho/a
left	izquierdo/a
sorry!	¡lo siento!
excuse me (can I get past?)	perdóneme
excuse me (can you help?)	por favor
sir, madam, miss	señor, señora, señorita
I don't understand	no comprendo
I would like . . .	quiero/quisiera . . .
large	grande
small	pequeño
do you have . . ?	¿tiene . . ?
please write it down	por favor, escríbalo

DAYS OF THE WEEK

Monday	lunes
Tuesday	martes
Wednesday	miércoles
Thursday	jueves
Friday	viernes
Saturday	sábado
Sunday	domingo

NUMBERS

0	cero
1	uno/a
2	dos
3	tres
4	cuatro
5	cinco
6	seis
7	siete
8	ocho
9	nueve
10	diez
11	once
12	doce
13	trece
14	catorce
15	quince
16	dieciséis
17	diecisiete
18	dieciocho
19	diecinueve
20	veinte
21	veintiuno
30	treinta
40	cuarenta
50	cincuenta
60	sesenta
70	setenta
80	ochenta
90	noventa
100	cien
101	ciento uno/a
200	doscientos/as
500	quinientos/as
1,000	mil
2,000	dos mil
1,000,000	un millón

Charco de los Clicos beach

Trasmediterránea, with offices in Arrecife, Lanzarote (*Tel: 928 811 188/ 928 824 930*) and Puerto del Rosario, Fuerteventura (*Tel: 928 850 877/ 928 850 095, fax: 928 852 476*).

Jet Foil also operates ferries with offices at Morro Jable, Fuerteventura (*Tel: 928 540 250; fax: 922 540 250*). The Trasmediterránea agent in Britain is **Southern Ferries**, 179 Piccadilly, London W1V 9DB (*Tel: (020) 7491 4968, fax: (020) 7491 3502*).

Ferries between Lanzarote and Fuerteventura are operated by **Fred Olsen**: Playa Blanca, Lanzarote (*Tel: 928 517 301*); Corralejo, Fuerteventura (*Tel: 928 535 090, www. fredolsen.es*); and by **Naviera Armas**: Arrecife, Lanzarote (*Tel: 928 811 037*);

Playa Blanca, Lanzarote (*Tel: 928 517 912/ 13*); Puerto del Rosario, Fuerteventura (*Tel: 928 851 542*); Corralejo, Fuerteventura (*Tel: 928 867 080, www.naviera-armas.com*).

The Thomas Cook *European Rail Timetable* (published monthly) has up-to-date details of ferry services; it is available to buy online at *www.thomascookpublishing.com*, from branches of Thomas Cook in the UK or phone (*01733) 416477*).

Buses
Bus services (buses are known as *guaguas*) operate on both islands, but their times are usually not useful for tourists, and they do not stop at many tourist sights. Central bus station

telephone numbers are as follows: Fuerteventura (*Tel: 928 850 951*), Lanzarote (*Tel: 928 811 546/928 812 458*).

Taxis

These are recognisable by a green light in the windscreen or on a white roof and an official plate with the letters SP, standing for *servicio público* (public service). The light shows *libre* (free) when they are available for hire. For short trips within tourist areas many cabbies won't bother to put their meters on, though you will rarely be cheated. Boards by the main taxi ranks display fixed prices between the most popular destinations. For longer distances, confirm the price before you start.

Senior citizens

Senior citizens are accorded discounts by some hotels on Lanzarote, but more often are only able to take advantage of long-stay discounts. Museums and attractions offer discounted admission.

Students and youth travel

The Canary Islands attract some backpacking youngsters, as seen in many other holiday islands throughout the world, but there are few official camping sites or youth hostels.

Sustainable tourism

Thomas Cook is a strong advocate of ethical and fairly traded tourism and believes that the travel experience should be as good for the places visited as it is for the people who visit them. That's why we firmly support The Travel Foundation, a charity that develops solutions to help improve and protect holiday destinations, their environment, traditions and culture. To find out what you can do to make a positive difference to the places you travel to and the people who live there, please visit *www.thetravelfoundation.org.uk*

Telephones

You can now make international calls from virtually any phone on the islands. The best way to phone home is from the *locutorias* (you'll find them almost everywhere), which have metered booths where you pay after your call, so you don't need change to hand. The LED indicator above your

Ferries operate between the islands

phone is not the amount in euros but the unit charge (which is considerably less). *Telefónicas* are generally in central locations and open late. Hotels usually levy a hefty surcharge. Calls are cheaper after 8pm.

For international calls, dial 00, wait for the tone to indicate that you have a line, then dial your country code (Australia 61, Canada and the USA 1, Ireland 353, UK 44), followed by the local code (omitting the first 0), then the number.

All the Canary Islands' telephone numbers now consist of nine digits. Those within the province of Las Palmas (Gran Canaria, Fuerteventura and Lanzarote) start with 928, and all nine digits must be dialled for all calls, including local ones. Spanish mobile-phone numbers also have nine digits.

Time

The Canaries maintain Greenwich Mean Time in the winter, which is one hour behind most European countries and in line with the UK. The clocks go ahead one hour in summer. The Canaries are five hours ahead of US Eastern Standard Time, and eight hours ahead of Pacific Time. Johannesburg is ahead by one hour, Australia by 10 hours and New Zealand by 12 hours.

Tipping

Most hotels and some restaurant bills include a service charge. A small tip (around 10 per cent) for a well-served meal, a friendly taxi driver, or hotel staff who have been particularly helpful will be appreciated. Don't forget to leave the hotel maid something, too.

Toilets

Public toilets are invariably very clean, with a few beach areas having a free public shower on the beach, and private showers/toilet facilities for a small fee. In order of preference, use those in

A bus travels through the edges of the Tremesana, Lanzarote

The tourist information office at Caleta de Fuste

CONVERSION TABLES

FROM	TO	MULTIPLY BY
Inches	Centimetres	2.54
Feet	Metres	0.3048
Yards	Metres	0.9144
Miles	Kilometres	1.6090
Acres	Hectares	0.4047
Gallons	Litres	4.5460
Ounces	Grams	28.35
Pounds	Grams	453.6
Pounds	Kilograms	0.4536
Tons	Tonnes	1.0160

To convert back, for example from centimetres to inches, divide by the number in the third column.

MEN'S SUITS

UK	36	38	40	42	44	46	48
Rest of Europe	46	48	50	52	54	56	58
USA	36	38	40	42	44	46	48

DRESS SIZES

UK	8	10	12	14	16	18
France	36	38	40	42	44	46
Italy	38	40	42	44	46	48
Rest of Europe	34	36	38	40	42	44
USA	6	8	10	12	14	16

MEN'S SHIRTS

UK	14	14.5	15	15.5	16	16.5	17
Rest of Europe	36	37	38	39/40	41	42	43
USA	14	14.5	15	15.5	16	16.5	17

MEN'S SHOES

UK	7	7.5	8.5	9.5	10.5	11
Rest of Europe	41	42	43	44	45	46
USA	8	8.5	9.5	10.5	11.5	12

WOMEN'S SHOES

UK	4.5	5	5.5	6	6.5	7
Rest of Europe	38	38	39	39	40	41
USA	6	6.5	7	7.5	8	8.5

hotels, restaurants and bars. Buy a drink in the latter as a matter of courtesy.

There are several terms for toilets: *servicios, aseos, WC, retretes*. The doors are usually marked *Señoras* (ladies) and *Caballeros* (gentlemen).

Tourist information

All the islands have a central tourist office (*turismo*), and the larger resorts have their own town offices (listed in *Destination guide* under the appropriate locations). Free maps and leaflets are usually on offer, together with bus timetables (not to be taken away) and sometimes other 'what's on' lists. All offices have at least one English-speaking member of staff, but the service you get depends very much on which member of staff you see. All offices should be able to help you with accommodation.

Before leaving home, contact your Spanish National Tourist Office:

Australia *203 Castlereagh Street, Level 2, Suite 21a, PO Box 675, 2000 Sydney NSW (Tel: (61) 2 264 7966).*

Canada *2 Bloor Street West, 14th Floor, Toronto, Ontario M5S 1M8 (Tel: (416) 961 3131).*

United Kingdom *22–23 Manchester Square, London W1M 5AP (Tel: (020) 7486 8077).*

USA *665 Fifth Avenue, New York, NY 10103 (Tel: (212) 759 88 22).*

Travellers with disabilities

There are wheelchair facilities at all the international air terminals, and as hotels and apartments continue to be built, more choice becomes available for the wheelchair user. Most of the wheelchair-equipped places to stay are in the newer resorts. For information from the UK, contact: **ATS Travel**, *1 Tankhill Road, Purfleet, Essex (Tel: (01708) 863198).* On Lanzarote in Puerto del Carmen is **Casas Heddy**, a Norwegian-inspired enterprise. (For details and bookings, write to: *Postboks 3083, Elisenberg 0207, Oslo 2, Norway.*)

General facilities throughout the islands are poor to nonexistent. There are very few adapted toilets, no adapted public transport facilities, nor adapted hire cars (even automatics are rare). Kerbs are high and the terrain is rough. The Spanish association for travellers with disabilities is **Federación ECOM**, *Gran Vía de las Corts Catalanes 562-2a, 08011, Barcelona (Tel: (932) 173 882).* UK travellers should contact the **Holiday Care Service** for their special factsheets on Lanzarote, and for any general advice: *2 Old Bank Chambers, Station Road, Horley, Surrey RH6 9HW (Tel: (01293) 774535).*

Few places are equipped with facilities for travellers with disabilities

Index

Acknowledgements

Thomas Cook wishes to thank the photographers, picture libraries and other organisations for the loan of the photographs reproduced in this book, to whom copyright in the photographs belongs.

BIG STOCK PHOTO/Quintessentia 185
BIG STOCK PHOTO/Alex Trefilov 87
CÉSAR-JAVIER PALACIOS 100, 121, 127, 169
FLICKR/Miss K 19, 39, zeitspuren 83, Michael Myers 137
PICTURES COLOUR LIBRARY 153
THOMAS COOK 1, 23, 24, 29, 53, 71, 73, 74, 97, 113, 119, 131, 145, 147, 157
WIKIMEDIA COMMONS/Yummifruitbat 69
WORLD PICTURES/PHOTOSHOT 34, 180

All remaining photographs were taken by STILLMAN ROGERS.

For CAMBRIDGE PUBLISHING MANAGEMENT LTD:
Project editor: Catherine Burch
Typesetter: Donna Pedley
Proofreader: Kelly Walker

SEND YOUR THOUGHTS TO
BOOKS@THOMASCOOK.COM

We're committed to providing the very best up-to-date information in our travel guides and constantly strive to make them as useful as they can be. You can help us to improve future editions by letting us have your feedback. If you've made a wonderful discovery on your travels that we don't already feature, if you'd like to inform us about recent changes to anything that we do include, or if you simply want to let us know your thoughts about this guidebook and how we can make it even better – we'd love to hear from you.

Send us ideas, discoveries and recommendations today and then look out for your valuable input in the next edition of this title.

Emails to the above address, or letters to Travellers Series Editor, Thomas Cook Publishing, PO Box 227, Coningsby Road, Peterborough PE3 8SB, UK.

Please don't forget to let us know which title your feedback refers to!